A SYMPOSIUM ON SLAVOJ ŽIŽEK: FAITH AND THE REAL

Edited by Elizabeth Wright and Edmond Wright

Contents

In Memoriam Elizabeth Wright

Eva Elizabeth Schloss was born in Würzburg, Bavaria, in 1926, the elder daughter of a Jewish family that was among the last to escape Germany after Kristallnacht and which eventually settled in Manchester. Here Elizabeth attended a Roman Catholic school (Loreto College) where she suffered an injustice that would seem to have contributed much to her constant suspicion of academic institutions. Although she was keen to pursue her education and had gained an excellent School Certificate, her school gave no encouragement for a return to the Sixth Form and also her parents were put under pressure by their British sponsors, who were not convinced of the value of university education for women, to get her into a job as soon as possible. She therefore trained as an art teacher at the then Manchester Regional College of Art and became a lecturer in textile design at Bolton College of Art. She married Edmond Wright in 1951 and in 1959 they both, dissatisfied with the education they had so far received, enrolled on external degree courses at the University of London, Edmond in philosophy and Elizabeth in English and German. Having gained a first class degree she embarked on doctoral research at Oxford, again with Edmond, and while both of their children were undergraduates at the same university. She was awarded her D.Phil. in 1976, owing much to her doctoral tutor Professor Siegbert Prawer, and her thesis on E.T.A. Hoffmann (which represented her first academic encounter with Freud) eventually became her first book, *E.T.A. Hoffmann and the Rhetoric of Terror: Aspects of Language used for the Evocation of Fear.* She became a college lecturer in German at St. Anne's College, Oxford, and taught there until she moved to Cambridge on being elected a Fellow at Girton College. Here she developed her interest further in the relations between psychoanalytic theory and literary criticism and in 1984 published her second and probably most influential book *Psychoanalytical Criticism: Theory in Practice.* A convincing demonstration of the interesting and liberating effects that can be produced when psychoanalysis and literature are brought into relations of mutual interaction, it also exemplifies Elizabeth's steadfast refusal to be waylaid by the polemical and ideological and her enduring and insistent assumption that if an idea is worth anything it can be expressed in such a way that anyone who was interested and willing to make some effort can understand and use it. A second revised edition was published in 1998 (*Psychoanalytic Criticism: A Reappraisal*) and it was awarded the Rose Mary Crawshay Prize by the British Academy.

This intellectual openness and fair-mindedness together with her passion for discussion, exposition and the making of connections continued to stand her in good stead as she turned to consider the difficult and often over-heated relations between feminist theory and psychoanalysis. The product of her work in this area was two collaborative volumes, *Feminism and Psychoanalysis: a Critical Dictionary* (1992) and *Coming out of Feminism?* (1998), in which she also began to engage with queer theory. By this time Lacan was her most important psychoanalytic interlocutor and she had become particularly impressed by the use made of Lacanian theory by Slavoj Žižek and the research group associated with him in Ljubljana, whose work exemplified intellectual values that had always been important to her. In 1999, *The Žižek Reader*, on which she had collaborated with Edmond, was published. In her last two books she continued and extended the three-way conversation between literature, psychoanalysis and feminist theory, *Speaking Desires can be Dangerous* (1999) and *Lacan and Postfeminism* (2000).

I met Elizabeth in 1996 when she and I were training as psycho-analysts at the Centre for Freudian Analysis and Research in London. We participated in two cartels together, one on Lacan's seminar on feminine sexuality and another on clinical work. From the start I was impressed by Elizabeth's openness and curiosity, her eagerness to engage in conversation and debate, to develop and extend ideas, her passion for making connections, and her remarkable physical and intel-lectual energy that, despite her age, always made her seem extremely youthful. I was also impressed by the fact that she was embarking on a long and often difficult clinical training after retiring from a varied and successful academic career and was thus moving against a trend that has concerned me for some time. Elizabeth and I often discussed what the academic commodification of psychoanalytic (particularly Lacanian) theory and the drift of Lacanians into the academy implied for psychoanalysis in this country as a specific social and political practice that seeks to establish and propagate conditions in which the psychoanalytic act can be effective. The discourse of the university (which is, after all, the discourse of the hatred induced by the impo-tence of knowledge) is the furthest removed from the discourse of the analyst, and Elizabeth's commitment to becoming a practising psycho-analyst, her fascination by the density, complexity and ethical heft of the clinical encounter, the seriousness and urgency with which she approached technical clinical questions, always impressed and heartened me and led me to think that the sub-title of her *Psychoanalytical Criticism* had become an imperative for her — *Theory in(to) Practice*. Just as she had resisted the appropriation of literature by psychoanalytic theory, so she resisted the appropriation of psychoanalytic theory by the academy, appropriations which in both cases implied a neutralisation of something uncomfortable, unsettling and dissident but, for these very reasons, important and salutary, essential even. During our last conversations the solemn academic elaboration of Lacanian readings of literature often became a light-hearted parlour game — *'And what about Iago?'* — *'Why, he's the analyst of course!'* — and I remember being struck by how much it meant to her when she became a full member of CFAR and how moved and grateful she was that she had finally found a place in an institution where she felt at ease, fully engaged with what interested her, and where she received full and appropriate recognition, a very different story from the way she felt about academic institutions, and, too, the psychoanalytical institutions that had refused to train her because of her age. Nevertheless, she always retained her strong sense of the importance and liberating power of education and the dignity and responsibility of the role of the educator, while in her training and practice as a psychoanalyst she resisted at every point anything and everything that smacked of imposture and the hieratic. As I think of her now this strong and consistent ethical demeanour is associated with the frequent and often rather opaque use she made of the word 'poetic,' as, for example, in her review of the curious book by Bice Benvenuto *The Rites of Psychoanalysis*, where she identifies as one of the strengths of the book its introduction of the poetic into the clinic. I have begun to think that what she meant by this could be understood as follows: if, as had usually been the case, the literary was on one side of Saussure's piece of paper as signifier while psychoanalytic theory was on the other as the signified, Elizabeth's characteristic manoeuvre, her poetic act, was to perform the half-twist that transforms the piece of paper into a Moebian surface, the Lacanian emblem of the irreducible subject; thus Elizabeth, who often doubted that she could ever be a 'true Lacanian,' showed herself more Lacanian, and indeed more Freudian, than many of those who today coquette with the modes of expression peculiar to those mighty thinkers and practitioners.

And this is what I will always remember of Elizabeth: her intellectual urgency and restlessness; her insistence that Saussure can have his piece of paper only as a Moebian surface, that individuals are never ultimately to be approached as tokens of types, that the subject and the ethical are irreducible, that gender is a matter of genre, that we must move from theory to praxis, from praxis to poesis, and back again; and in particular her alertness to the ethical implications of any given theoretical position, her quick, almost raw sensitivity to the points where discourses of liberation themselves become opaque and oppressive.

WAYNE BARRON

Introduction: Faith and the Real

We believe that this volume of *Paragraph* represents the first collection of critical responses to be made to the work of Slavoj Žižek. It draws from a variety of engaged readers of his prolific output, judging it from philosophical, political, cultural and psychoanalytical viewpoints. From the editorial stance it is particularly fortunate that three of the contributors, Terry Eagleton, Bran Nicol and Kenneth Reinhard, have here together in their differing ways given introductions to his work, and so as editors we can refer the reader to their articles for a survey of his concerns, his methods and his reception. This unusually gives us the space to draw attention to a particular feature of his thought, the centrality of the notion of the Real. This volume of *Paragraph* should display this connection across the diversity of fields that he covers while at the same time showing the versatility of its relevance.

It is with Lacan's concept of the Real above all that Žižek has brought psychoanalysis to bear on fields traditionally kept apart. The Real is one of Lacan's three 'Orders,' the Real, the Symbolic and the Imaginary, a tripartite map of the relations existing among the body (and, indeed nature generally), the language that fashions a body into a socialized being, and the efforts of fantasy to assuage the structurally inescapable inadequacies of that fashioning. That this eliciting of subjecthood from an intractable material should produce paradoxes appears suspect to the rational mind reared on the logical clarities of the Enlightenment. What, for example, is one to make of such a typical declaration from Žižek as that the subject can only recognize itself through acknowledging what it cannot recognize?[1] It is this kind of conundrum from Žižek, and his master Jacques Lacan, that sends the clear-minded among us wincing away, or, more usually, apportioning such enigmas to easy neglect. As Terry Eagleton notes at the end of his article, most English philosophers have never heard of Slavoj Žižek, much less are able to pronounce his name (his first name pronounced 'Slavoy' and his surname with the two 'Z's' pronounced like the 'S' in 'measure').

In order to allay some suspicion we are therefore going to use our editorial space to present a *philosophical* approach to the Real and the strategies of the Symbolic to attempt to grasp it. This concentration upon the Real, it is hoped, should provide the reader with an effectual entry into all the articles, and thus enable us to introduce them without the more customary mini-summaries. This approach concerns specifically the strategy persons spontaneously and unthinkingly pursue when drawn into the dialogue that is language.

It was said by Kant long ago that

> To one man, for instance, a certain word suggests one thing, to another some other thing; the unity of consciousness in that which is empirical is not, as regards what is given, necessarily and universally valid. (*Critique of Pure Reason*, B140)

This uncontentious statement, that it is not possible for two persons' understandings to match exactly, has not been given by philosophers the attention it deserves. Fortunately, a psycholinguist with a special interest in communication, Ragnar Rommetveit, has concerned himself with this very matter; he has empirically established the fact that it is possible for two persons to arrive at practical co-ordination in speech and action without either being aware that they each have marked differences of perception and understanding.[2] These differences would, indeed, only become salient to one or both in some entirely new context unforeseen by either, in which some hidden criterion on which one had been unconsciously relying became relevant to his or her current purposes. A logician, Harry S. Leonard, has commented on this universal feature of communication, an ever-present but concealed 'misapprehension':

> Two people engaged in this same process of trying to reach a common understanding may well find two sets of criteria which remarkably well isolate the same extension. But do they understand the word in the same way?[3]

Notice a radical implication here which goes beyond his remark and that of Kant's: the two might not even be using criteria that pick out strictly the same extension, the same 'thing'. For one of them, his 'entity' might not be considered to last as long as the other's 'entity,' or cease to be 'the same thing' when it changes in some quality (say, in colour, weight or taste). As Aristotle commented, what are six apples for the seller do not necessarily count as six apples for the buyer.

But Leonard's remark can take us further: it does not matter (in the sense of how the participants in language judge their intentions and how they direct their separate attentions) whether their attempts at co-ordination do coincide fully, that is, each might have their own 'entity,' their own selection from the individual experiences they are having, as long as the 'failure' of overlap between these selections does not immediately interfere with their judgements of success in the action concerned. The implication is a startling one: there is actually *no single entity in front of them at all — its 'singularity' is something supposed for the convenience of communication.* That convenience is established by each behaving as if their two selections from experience actually *did* coincide. Obviously, if they did not make this necessary but strictly false assumption that there was only 'one' entity in front of them, they could never bring their separate judgements into any sort of harness.

To make this plainer, the structure involved is of a similar character to that of two persons talking over the phone about something they both happen to be watching on television. There may be distinct differences in the quality of the pictures on the screen (e.g. in the colour settings or the size of the screen), but both persons refer to the 'same object' that they pick out (even though that quality difference might, unknown to them both, be significant for what they are talking about — say, in a programme about art, a painting). A word may be, as V. N. Vološinov put it, 'a territory shared by addresser and addressee,'[4] but it is not quite the same territory for them both.

This assumption of there being a single entity, furthermore, is sustained by judgements of how far current intentions are being fulfilled, and intentions themselves are notoriously open to indefinite exploration. The sociologist Harold Garfinkel speaks of the 'Et Cetera' principle,[5] which states that all communication makes use of the assumption that, though not everything has been strictly defined for some present statement, there is a vague region of relevance which supposed to be the same for each participant — when it patently is not. Linguists such as Sir Alan Gardiner,[6] and philosophers of science such as Michael Polanyi[7] have stressed that intention has depths beyond the conceptualizing of the agent. Even analytical philosophers have drawn attention to this characteristic of intention, one calling it 'The Accordion Effect'[8] because the intentional description of an act can be widened without limit. Why did you have that cup of tea in that café? — not merely because you were thirsty, not merely because you wanted a rest, not merely because you were waiting for someone, etc., etc.

A sociologist, Alfred Schutz, reached the same conclusion as Rommetveit, arguing that, in order for two persons to engage in the co-operative act that is communication, they have to perform something that is not actually the case, namely, to behave as if, were they able to exchange their perspectives on the world — stand in the other's shoes, so to speak, thus seeing the world as their partner in dialogue does — then the object or whatever in front of them would appear *exactly the same*. He called it 'the Idealization of Reciprocity,' the assumption of 'an interchangeability of standpoints'.[9] This is precisely what the very first two philosophers to glimpse this key structure noted. They were both American, Roy Wood Sellars and Clarence Irving Lewis: 'No two individuals can possibly have numerically the same thing-experiences, even though it works ordinarily to make that assumption';[10] 'the possibility of agreement' in our acting together in the world must be 'antecedently presumed'.[11]

Rommetveit, independently of Schutz, puts it this way: 'we must, naively and unreflectively, take the possibility of perfect intersubjectivity for granted in order to achieve partial intersubjectivity in real-life discourse with our fellow-men'.[12] And in case anyone should think that the phrase 'take for granted' means *actually be convinced of,* one only has to analyse the phrase; 'take for' means *to accept an partial confirmation for a full one* or *to accept an appearance for reality,* as in the sentence 'It was so foggy I took him for his brother'; and 'to grant' means *to assent, to allow, to permit to be realized,* which clearly implies a matter concerning our will, decision, desire, fear. So 'take for granted' means *to accept for the time being that something not fully confirmed will be treated as such according to our judgement of our current purposes.*

Next step. A difference relevant for one person A and not for the other B that has *not* surfaced into mutual acknowledgement lies in a peculiar region of awareness. It may be something sensed which has not even been commonly attended to by anyone other than A; indeed, it may not even have been named in the public language. As Wilhelm von Humboldt put it:

All understanding is simultaneously a noncomprehension; all agreement in ideas and emotions is at the same time a divergence.[13]

What is *implicit* for each cannot all be *explicit* for both. Of two persons A and B, A herself is certainly not aware of this difference in her experience from that of B. Though it may be also sensed by B, it has not been brought to his attention, and therefore, while he is sensing perfectly well, he does not know what it is he is sensing that has the significance A is attributing to it. He has no idea that she is making any such attribution because there is nothing in the current discussion to make it salient. As C. I. Lewis put it:

It is, thus, quite possible that we may understand each other perfectly when we should disagree about the definition of our terms, because only some restricted meaning, covered in both our definitions, is required by our discussion.[14]

Sensing and knowing, therefore, come apart in a division that is not recognized in the public language. Person A is using a word with that criterion as part of her application of it, but no one else is so doing. Tomorrow it may turn out, because of some mismatch in behaviour, that the difference comes to public recognition, and clearly it is possible that difference may emerge as beneficial to all (it may even be person B who discovers that A is using the word differently from everyone else, so it would be A's insight but B's discovery!).

But now we can see a more radical conclusion still: since no one's sensing is the same as anyone else's (a fact undisputed by neurophysiologists), and since no one attends to precisely the same sensory features of the world as anyone else, it is empirically impossible for the common word to capture all that is being experienced by those who are engaging in communication. As the philosopher of rhetoric Hans-Georg Gadamer has put it, there is always 'the infinity of the unsaid'.[15] We project the illusion of finitude upon the infinite. Of course, one can say that, strictly speaking, we do not know whether the Real consists of discrete elements or is a continuum or is a mixture of both (consider the physicists' continuing debate about 'wave' or 'particle'), but what is obvious is that in order to inform someone of something we have to behave *as if* the world consisted of finite, discrete 'dry-goods,' to use J. L. Austin's phrase.

Communication thus turns out to require a 'naïve and unreflective' projection of agreement on supposedly discrete portions selected from individually separate fields of experience, an agreement that can never reach a logically perfect coincidence of understanding. Although Speaker and Hearer must, as Rommetveit and Schutz insist, assume a perfect agreement over 'whatever they refer to', this is only a useful, *unconscious* method of obtaining such co-ordination as they can manage. To quote Gadamer again, 'this dialectic of reciprocity that governs all "I-Thou" relationships is inevitably hidden from the mind of the individual'.[16] Once this is established in any ongoing statement that is being made in the real world, then an adjustment of that agreement can be made and the Hearer's concept be updated, that is, the initially agreed finite boundaries are moved about on the in-finite. As was said above, unless we acted as if we made *perfect* reference to 'single objects and persons,' we could never maintain the *partial* overlap that is necessary if we are to do any updating at all, which is, after all, the purpose of speech. To use Saussurean terms, we have to perform the *synchronic* perfection of language is order to allow the *diachronic* correction to go through.

To put the human situation of language in another way; both participants have their own selection in front of them which they call 'the entity,' but *it is not the same portion of the Real for each of them.* That is both entities are real — in the sense that they exist as separate individual selections from existence — but they are not numerically the same selection for A and B. Indeed, if they (impossibly) were identical, there would be no point in speaking, which is to adjust our references upon the world. So see how easy it is to slip into being convinced that the objective is real, for one's own selection *is* from the Real — what we forget is that, however objective we may think it to be, it is not the same bit of the Real that the other is selecting. Thus the conclusion is that, *objectivity*, that would-be safe agreement about entities in the world (including persons and selves), is not to be identified with *existence*. Existence remains uncaptured by language even when all parties profess themselves satisfied: objectivity is but an aspect of the needful Idealization of Reciprocity, our 'faith' in which is sustained by all the testing we have done with that 'entity' to date. Sensing is never perceiving, which implies that our unconscious 'faith' in 'perfect objectivity' is never without risk. All entities therefore, constructed from the Real though they are, have a virtual quality, remaining forever provisional. In Rommetveit's words,

we cannot attain closure and assess propositional content without prejudging a multifaceted, only partially known and opaque 'reality'.[17]

This opacity is that of the Real. In addition, we need the co-operation of all members of the speaking group to produce the best possible outcome, for the 'truth' can clearly be in the possession of the least 'authoritative' member, to whom authority should pass like a baton in a race. Nearly two thousand years ago Sextus Empiricus warned us that 'truth is a rare thing and on this account it is possible for one man to be wiser than the majority'.[18] To give a current statement of the same view, as Alain Badiou puts it, 'truth can appear as boring a hole in the encyclopaedia [of knowledges]'.[19]

Many an analytical philosopher has protested against such conclusions. To take an up-to-date example out of innumerable cases, in a new book on the philosophy of perception Michael Tye refines on a theory he has earlier proposed called 'representationalism'. What is noteworthy is that in defining it he confidently begins with the commonsense experience of having familiar objects in front of him; he believes we start with 'how *things* look to you';[20] (my italics). He nowhere inquires into how that identification was achieved or intersubjectively maintained and never questions the possibility that there actually could be no logically single entities to be seen, that our sensory experience could be no more than bare evidence. He also believes that a sensory experience is 'publicly accessible' in an *identical* way to everyone.[21] But sensory experience is bare in the sense of needing the drive of pleasure and pain to deem it significant at all. Imagine a mutation in some advanced animal, say, a monkey, born with perfect seeing, hearing, smelling, etc., but no feelings of pleasure and pain. It is obvious that the monkey could gain no knowledge whatsoever. Or imagine the reverse, it born with feelings of pleasure and pain but no other senses (this would be *jouissance* at its most blind): equally there could be no knowledge. In both cases, there would be evidence but no possibility of making use of it. Our experience does not 'represent the world': it merely gives us *evidence* that we may or not take advantage of.

That experience, both the sensory and that of pleasure and pain, is part of the Real, just as bare, even 'brute' or 'raw' as philosophers say, as what causes it, other parts of the Real. Consider this analogy: a piece of rock falls from a cliff, bounces into some clay, and flies off to land yards away. It leaves behind a near-perfect imprint of one side of itself in the clay. Is this a 'representation' of the rock? No, of course not; it is just a freak occurrence as contingent as anything else. Similarly with what happens when a distribution of light-rays arrive at your retinas; things happen automatically in the evolved brain and an 'imprint' of sorts becomes your experience of that whole distribution. But the significance of the variations within that distribution have to be, as we say, 'painfully' learned. And we can go on learning more and more. Inspector Morse on seeing the *evidence* of a footprint might at first say that 'someone has been here'; then, 'a man has been here'; then 'a man with a limp has been here'; then, 'an exceptionally tall man has been here,' etc., etc. The Real is infinite, remaining outside the Symbolic even when we are experiencing it. So we have to say 'We *sense* the Real, but *know* only those precarious and tentative selections we have made from it with the help of our motivation system, and — since we are human and can communicate with each other — with the help of what we have learned from the Symbolic, held in place by our mutual trust (and our luck with the Real so far)'. Existence is what we sense, and it is always there, known or unknown; the so-called 'real world' of objects and persons and named properties is actually only a possible world, for any of these guesses might fail us at any time. Logicians believe that they can imagine 'possible worlds' when the fact is we really live in one. So when Eagleton amusingly writes here that Lacanians see the objective world as 'just a low-grade place of fantasy in which we shelter from the terrors of the Real,' he is not far from the truth. Dr. Samuel Johnson kicked a stone thinking to disprove Berkeley's idealism thereby, but he only demonstrated the *existence* of 'what' he felt with his foot, for what he kicked might not have been 'a stone' at all, but a projection of some rock, or a brick, or some partly buried iron, etc., etc. If everyone there were agreed that 'it' *was* a stone, that would have been a confirmation of the idealized reciprocity of him and his fellows in the dialogue of the ongoing Symbolic Order. When Berkeley said that all objects remained the same because they are 'seen by God,' *he was ironically correct*, for the singularity of 'the stone' is projected by the naïve mutual 'faith' — which we can call 'God' if we like.

What are such philosophers as Tye actually doing when they insist on the objectivity of things and properties (e.g. believing that a scent is 'publicly accessible' in an *identical* way for all)? To answer this, a kind of *argumentum ad hominem* is for once justifiable. To be convinced that there exist observable discrete entities (and definable properties) in the Real as an axiom of one's *philosophical* argument is to remain inside the Idealization of Reciprocity *without being aware that one is.* So therefore to insist, as for example, with David Wiggins, that 'the object is there anyway,'[22] is no more than to encourage us to apply the Idealization of Reciprocity, to join with him in the unreflective 'faith' that sustains language. And who could complain about that — *at the level of ordinary speech*? So he is not speaking as *a philosopher*, one who should be examining the basis of dialogic communication: he is still at the level of *the ordinary speaker* without knowing it. It is just the same mistake when he says that all our separate vaguenesses about an object 'match exactly,'[23] for what is hidden from mutual understanding is undoubtedly different for each participant, but we have to behave as if it is not, and this last is really what he is telling us to do, to engage in the 'naïve and unreflective' faith. He does not see that to say that one person's vagueness is the same as another's is equivalent to saying we must neglect all that we separately consider negligible, and this is plainly an *exhortation* to take the supposed 'singularity' of 'the entity' for granted. But there is no doubt that we cannot know that what is 'negligible' for you is 'negligible' for me; tomorrow we may find it was not. This is what all stories are about. This ambiguity is betrayed in the common phrase 'to all intents and purposes': when we say 'we shall treat something as something else to all intents and purposes,' we know it actually means the opposite of that, that there is a certain doubt about the equivalence, but it will do for the time being. And this is precisely what we do for any entity — the human co-ordination of a pair of guesses (that actually produces 'it' by treating the two as a single certainty) will work for the time being. It is like using money and knowing how to bargain (and *thus alter its value*), instead of, like a miser, fetishizing it.

So this error such philosophers are making can become a very dangerous because it ignores three things: first, the *hypothetical* nature of the Idealization; second, the fact that it depends on what has the structure of a *trust* between two persons; and third, it not only ignores the risk involved but tries to turn the trust into *a superstitious conviction* that words do in fact fit the world. This complacent assertion — when the world is plainly rife with unpleasant surprises — turns the Idealization, which is only after all a method (that enables us together to hold a portion of the Real roughly in place) into an occult dogma. At its worst it turns into an insistence on one's own preferred interpretation of some identity or other, an attitude basically narcissistic and authoritarian, whether one is tyrannically at the centre of the social order or anarchistically at the periphery of it. This is what Žižek repeatedly warns against, the turning of the Law into an obsessional fixity, the perverse obedience one finds in ascesis, for example, or the comic example of Hašek's 'Good Soldier Schweik,' who threw the Austrian army into confusion by following his orders with absolute precision.[24] Žižek borrows Kant's fantasy[25] in which a man is allowed a vision of the Divine Order, the result being that he is turned into a lifeless puppet.[26] We can now perhaps see a way as to why, to use Terry Eagleton's phrase, 'language is not all there is'.

To keep to theological terminology, such philosophers are not being 'religious' in Kierkegaard's sense; that is, they are behaving as if the language is in perfect order as it is and requires no adjustment from individual subjects. The whole point of a religious faith, if we are to accept Žižek's interpretation of St. Paul, is to view the existing Law, both legal and moral, as something to be reshaped, not in the sense of a disobedient reaction, but as a transformation of *both* subject *and* law. For an explanation of Žižek here see Michael Moriarty's contribution in this volume, where St. Paul is taken as encouraging us to break out 'of the vicious superego cycle of the Law and its transgression'.[27] This is the Kierkegaardian faith that 'cannot even be externalized into the universal medium of language',[28] and why not? — because the whole point of speaking is *to change the language*. This is the real message of the Cretan Liar story, in that we are all strictly 'liars' as soon as we have something new to say, for to utter any informative statement *does change the language, albeit perhaps only infinitesimally*. The linguist Sir Alan Gardiner, in opposition to Saussure's 'superstitious' over-reliance on the negations of the Symbolic structure, points out that the living ox before two French observers does make its own new, positive, if infinitesimal, contribution to the *signifié* of the word *boeuf*.[29] It is where the Symbolic Order of language gains by accretion from the Real.

The only kind of languages that are not provisional are those of pure logic and pure mathematics, for in them we have decided for the nonce to treat them as if they will never refer to the Real, that is, nothing can ever alter the meaning of the signs we use within them. Evidence of this can be found in the fact that, as soon as we try to refer while still believing ourselves in the realm of the non-referring, paradoxes result. Zeno's paradoxes, for example, all depend on the impossible reference to something so small that no mutual agreement about that portion as a part of the Real could ever be reached (this point was made in 1836 by Alexander Bryan Johnson[30]). The paradox in Gödel's Proof of the Inconsistency of Mathematics arises because it contains an illicit attempt to refer, namely, in making numbers refer to other numbers. Treating numbers as never referring makes them of course the most fictive of all uses of language: ordinary words may only refer by virtue of our mutual idealization, but at least they retain a current tenuous hold on the Real. In pure mathematics the *logos* becomes pure *mythos*.

The question of the 'faith' of the Idealization of Reciprocity requires a closer look. If the 'faith' is 'naïve and unreflective,' then it does not in itself partake of any moral worth. After all, one can talk with an enemy — even though it creates an odd irony that two enemies must to that minimal level agree together. But what obviously does happen that a *genuine* faith can be consciously built on the *naïve* foundation, one that openly acknowledges the risk that is attendant upon it. This in turn implies that those one loves can never be wholly as one believes; they are irredeemably alien, a part of the opaque Real — indeed, it can be said that they are therefore to an unknown degree one's 'enemies,' whom one has, nevertheless, to love. But — and this is Žižek's repeated insistence — the self just as much contains an alien core or 'kernel' that, though it constitutes the Real inside one, remains ever detached from the mutual definitions within which we have created our very subjecthood (through what

Althusser named its 'interpellations', the 'calls' that elicited the self from the undivided Real, which, being a part of the Symbolic, cannot just work one way; for a discussion of Althusser's notion, again see Moriarty).

To imagine that the Symbolic Order of language guarantees one's own interpretations of it is to be narcissistically lost, whether one is speaking from the standpoint of the 'authorities' (like Kierkegaard's 'ethical' stage where a formal code is taken as guide) or from that of the anarchic rebel (like his 'aesthetic' one, where a supposed 'inner' light is the source of action). To be positivist about entities is thus to be superstitious, even bigoted, and Žižek would say that the motivation is that of the 'obscene superego,' the investing of the Law with uncontrolled *jouissance*. Instead of the entrance to the Symbolic being a faith that allows for the endless risk of semantic correction, that is, admitting the likelihood of a sacrifice of *jouissance*, it is taken as a boundless reassurance and permission. What should be, 'a shared ignorance,' as Žižek calls it[31] — which, incidentally, is a good description of one aspect of the Idealization of Reciprocity — is colonized as an absolute knowledge. In contrast to this, there is the example of Antigone that Lacan examined, here discussed by Russell Grigg. Her case is especially interesting because it shows an attempt to assert an 'absolute freedom,' but, as Grigg argues, though 'every act is a crime' set against the perfection of the Law, no one can be free of having to restructure the Symbolic, to move what Lacan called the *points de capiton*, the upholstery buttons that roughly hold the Symbolic to the Real. From the point of view of a perfect Symbolic, however, any such attempt would be, as Eagleton notes, 'Original Sin,' but, since one can privilege neither Symbolic nor Real, the Symbolic is just as much of an original sin against the subject. It is the Cretan Liar structure showing itself again: one hopes to move *within* the language *to change* the language. My own comment here has been to note that this implies that both comedy and tragedy are actual possibilities as life-structures for both subject and society, which makes the hopeful acceptance of risk in the public faith all the more fraught.[32] If this should be the case, then it is not 'an obscene vision of humanity,' as Eagleton puts it, that Žižek is presenting: it is rather that we should adopt Thomas Hardy's warning — 'if way to the Better there be, it exacts a full look at the Worst' ('In tenebris, II,' line 14).

And here we have come round to the theme of Žižek's most recent books, *The Ticklish Subject* and *The Fragile Absolute*, for they deal above all with how the relation of the Symbolic to the Real underlies our major present political and moral concerns. If 'sharing a language' is only a co-ordinating of unsure overlaps, then Žižek's paradoxes begin to make sense. To take the one with which we began, that 'the subject can only recognize itself through acknowledging what it cannot recognize'.[33] If what is at the core of our bodily being is a kernel of the Real — as 'bare evidence' — that forever escapes the publicly 'shared' language by which we seek to understand it, then to acknowledge that alien experience, 'to recognize' it, is inevitably to realize that we cannot wholly capture it in words, that is, 'not to recognize it'. This is easy to understand if we accept that we can sense what we cannot ultimately know. As Roy Wood Sellars used to insist, 'being is one thing and knowledge is another,'[34] which, in Lacanese, is 'The Real is one thing and the Symbolic is another'. Žižek himself says something, another paradox, which can now be seen to be the equivalent of this:

This dialectical procedure of how an entity can *become* X only on so far as it has to renounce *being* X is precisely what Lacan calls "symbolic castration", the gap between the symbolic place and the element which fills it, the gap on account of which an element can *fill* its place only in so far as it *is not* directly this place'.[35]

The 'symbolic place' is the mutually idealized *identity* of our separate selections from the Real, and the Real provides 'the element' that 'fills' it, for each of us *differently*. Slavoj Žižek's own contribution to this volume, concerned with the films of Krzysztof Kieslowski, can be said to centre on the problem of the subject's encounter with the Real, both in itself as 'object' and with the other. He sees the films as presenting versions of a 'not-yet-constituted universe', where rival fantasies strive in conflict, those fantasies to which subjects depend for their very subjecthood, which are endeavours to hide the failure of the Symbolic to define them, that failure Lacan terms the 'Void' or the 'Lack'. The failure to accept that 'shared ignorance' extends to the sexual relationship, for which Lacan used the hyperbole of 'the impossibility of the sexual relationship,' as 'impossible' as any other identification. Kieslowski's play of doubles in film after film takes that impossibility as its very topic.

The virtuality of the subject takes on a peculiar intensity when exposed to the performances of cyberspace. The symbolic pact of language reveals its necessary risk with a special character in the exchanges of the chat-rooms. As Jerry-Ann Flieger points out, as in the Joke and the Riddle — and in the tragedy of that riddler Oedipus — 'laws are broken and re-established simultaneously,' performing the same structure as in St. Paul's recommendation. As she puts it 'meaning is up for grabs between player and umpire'. It is appropriate that Flieger uses the Joke pattern throughout her article to make a critique of Žižek's own foray into the cultural significance of communication in cyberspace, which itself was partly in response on one of Flieger's.

The functioning of Symbolic faith, according to Žižek, is at the core of today's political and international troubles. Global capitalism is parasitic upon the culture of individual nations and social groups, both in the sense of colonizing their values and aesthetic character and yet in the process inevitably erasing those very differences. What is being erased is the level of genuine symbolic faith, one that not only tolerated risk but expected and coped with it. There has been a consequent increase in the level of superstition, the turning to creeds, political and religious, that promise full control, the absence of risk. Fear-driven, and thus cowardly, they insidiously direct *jouissance* under the guise of obedience. As Žižek asserts in his latest book, on totalitarianism,[36] the fascist or Stalinist leader obtains the apparent loyalty of his subjects by presenting rape and violence, not as transgressions, but as things commanded by the law, even, as was the case with the Nazis, presented as sacrifices of 'normal decency' for the greater cause. Jason Glynos explores this 'decline of symbolic efficiency' as a result of globalization, seeing that it is precisely mutual trust that becomes a casualty. Instead of the Symbolic Order, the 'big Other,' being socially created as a focus of an essentially unrealizable hope, it is misrecognized as having a foundation in the Real. Hence the paranoid distortions such as New-Age cults, extreme fundamentalisms, suicidal sects, UFO societies and their like, all of which are seeking an 'Other of the Other,' a supposedly Real support in the face of the felt loss of a genuine trust. Kenneth Reinhard makes plain Žižek's point that the subject who is unable to accept the risk projects his fear outward such that a scapegoat becomes the imagined thief of his *jouissance*, intensifying the aggressivity of his racism and xenophobia.

When Bran Nicol speaks of the necessity of ideology, as something 'valuable' and 'perfectly normal,' he can be said to be pointing to the need for the maintenance of the Idealization of Reciprocity. Within the philosophy presented here, it is a matter of recognizing that the Symbolic already depends on its 'naïve and unreflecting' faith. This, though not of itself a support for hope, can nevertheless give us ground for optimism in that we can regain the trust that blindly sustained the best communities in the past by consciously *performing* what they did unthinkingly and which everyone who speaks is still doing.

The worst aspects of religion and nationalism in the past, the massacres of so-called 'intolerance,' were the result of the scapegoating Reinhard identifies. But, as Žižek is arguing is his latest books, some kind of return to symbolic faith is required if we are to escape a repetition of such history. At worst, religion has been relegated to the schools, where it may hold a sentimental Santa Claus status or has vanished into a multicultural history of religions. Patriotism has been given a bad name by Hitler; we seem to think it is the kind of thing William Hague waves in his speeches. Liberal politicians often say that they are patriotic, but patriotism does not make its appearance in their serious pronouncements of policy; on the contrary, they are visibly embarrassed by mention of it, believing, for those in England, that it is going to undermine their wanting to join the Euro and their wishing to keep England somehow in its ghost position as still imperial within the United Kingdom (witness New Labour's fear of a separate parliament for England with a *federal* parliament for England, Scotland and Wales). We need a recognition of a national polity that does not require the hatred of asylum-seekers, homosexuals, Pakistanis, black people, or Jews to maintain it, but, on the contrary, draws them into the common faith. What is required is the open acknowledgement of there having to be a common hope, maintained by poetic creation and renewal of a culture that celebrates the place and all who live in it. Some theorists of nationalism persist in being suspicious of the 'invention' of national culture: they can only see it as a kind of 'noble lie' in Plato's sense, in which an elite cynically encourage a religion in which they do not believe and the plebs as cynically reject it with what Peter Sloterdijk calls 'kynicism' (Sloterdijk, 1988). But what is required is a lie that is really noble *because everyone takes a part in it knowing not to be true.* Where Pascal (see Moriarty) thought that all you had to do to be religious was to go through the motions and belief would follow, the proper approach is to go through the motions with *everyone* knowing that belief *will never follow.* This is why Žižek need not be so suspicious of irony and laughter,[37] because one must encourage everyone *to play seriously* in the social language, well aware of the risk. This was V. N. Vološinov's/Michael Bakhtin's counsel: discourse must maintain 'a double focus'.[38] There have been minds still under the Enlightenment's influence who are unable to play. Ernst Cassirer rejected the idea of such a religion: 'without belief in the reality of its object, myth would lose its ground';[39] but to make that very utterance he had to hold to the Idealization of Reciprocity, which is precisely to perform a myth of there being 'objects'. Jean Baudrillard has noted that when the Iconoclasts broke the idols (and recall the Talibans' recent destruction of the Buddha statues) what they really could not stand was the truth that God was no more than his image.[40] Consider also the protests within the Church of England at the 'heretical' theology of Don Cupitt, who recommends behaving as if there is a God while knowing full well that there is not.[41] This is surely Žižek's 'shared mode of disidentification,' in which the community has to maintain 'a *proper distance* towards the object'.[42]

Such an argument is traceable back to its roots in the Lacanian view of the subject's construction in language, to the originary failure of the Symbolic to capture the Real within and without. When Lacan says that the satisfactory end of an analysis is a 'subjective destitution,' he means that the analysand has come to recognise that his identity cannot be encompassed by the Symbolic, in Žižek's words, that one 'freely assumes one's non-existence,' a hyperbole that in the relevant sense is hardly a hyperbole at all, since the mundane 'reality' of one's subjecthood is precisely what has to be put in question. To reach the end of an analysis one has 'to traverse the fantasy,' that is, one has to regain something of the fundamental act of the imagination that brought the subject into existence in the first place. That originary moment in which the 'pre-linguistic imagination' produced the fundamental fantasy that grounded the subject as a subject cannot of itself be relived, but its effects can be brought within the reach of some control. Language draws a subject into existence by projecting a promise of final fulfilment at the impossible conclusion of its naming of the world, and each subject creates a fantasy, drawn from some chance encounter in infancy, Freud's 'unary trait,' that acts to conceal that impossibility. This is the 'sublime object,' the *objet petit a*, as Lacan terms it, that at once hides and betrays the failure of language to deliver the Real as named and defined. It is like the promise on a banknote to pay the bearer 'the pound': language will work as money does, that is, as long as no one takes the promise seriously (as the American cult the 'Promise-Keepers' seem to believe[43]) — or becomes a cynic about it (as during hyperinflation). Just as with money it is the judgement of separate subjects that takes its value up and down as long as they join in the semblance of a common value, so too the negotiation of our desires in communication depends on our judgement of the meaning of the words we use. Though we cannot help trying to making our desire that of the Other, the Real in each of us will produce a change, infinitesimal or momentous, in the meanings of the words we use to express it. As Žižek puts it, the Lacanian avoids in language the Scylla of cynical distance and the Charybdis of unquestioning belief by 'counting on the efficiency of the big Other without trusting it,'[44] which is as much as to say that there should be a faith in its deliverances that turns into neither the nihilism of the former nor the superstition of the latter. This is why Žižek calls psychoanalysis a 'vanishing mediator,' a catalyst, between *logos* and *mythos*, between the logical perfection of the Symbolic Order with its Parmenidean world ordered by the public Word, and the fantasy of the private bliss of consummatory *jouissance* in a Plotinian One. The racist behaves as if these opposites can be fused. To be emancipated is to keep them in dialectical play.

EDMOND WRIGHT
University of Cambridge

NOTES

1 Slavoj Žižek, *The Fragile Absolute — Or Why is the Christian Legacy worth fighting For?* (London, Verso, 2000), p. 28.

2 Ragnar Rommetveit, *On Message Structure: A Framework for the Study of Language and Communication* (London, John Wiley and Sons, 1974).

3 Harry S. Leonard, *Principles of Reasoning: An Introduction to Logic, Methodology and the Theory of Signs* (New York, Dover Publications, 1967), p. 266.

4 V. N. Vološinov, *Marxism and the Philosophy of Language*, trans. Ladislav Metejka and I. R. Titunik (New York, Seminar Press, 1973), p. 86.

5 Harold Garfinkel, 'Studies in the Routine Ground of Everyday Activities'. *Social Problems*, 11 (1964), 220–50 (pp. 247–8).

6 Sir Alan Gardiner, *The Theory of Speech and Language* (Oxford, Oxford University Press, 1932).

7 Michael Polanyi, *Knowing and Being*, ed. Marjorie Greene (London, Routledge, 1969).

8 Joel Feinberg, 'Action and Responsibility' in *Philosophy in America*, ed. Max Black (London, Allen and Unwin, 1964), pp. 134–60.

9 Alfred Schutz, *Collected Papers, Vol. I: The Problem of Social Reality* (The Hague, Martinus Nijhoff, 1962), pp. 3–47.

10 Roy Wood Sellars, *Critical Realism: A Study of the Nature and Conditions of Knowledge* (Chicago and New York, Rand McNally, 1916).

11 Clarence Irving Lewis, *Mind and the World-Order* (London, Charles Scribner's Sons, 1929), p. 21.

12 Ragnar Rommetveit, 'On Negative Rationalism in Scholarly Studies of Verbal Communication and Dynamic Residuals in the Construction of Human Intersubjectivity,' in *The Social Contexts of Method*, eds. Michael Brenner, P. Marsh and Marilyn Brenner (London, Croom Helm, 1978), pp. 16–32 (p. 31).

13 Wilhelm von Humboldt, *Linguistic Variability and Intellectual Development*, trans. George C. Buck and Frithjof Raven (Coral Gables, Florida, University of Miami Press, 1971), p. 43.

14 Lewis, *Mind and the World-Order*, p. 85.

15 Hans-Georg Gadamer, *Truth and Method*, eds. and trans. Garrett Barden and John Cumming (London, Sheed and Ward, 1975; orig. pub. J. C. B. Mohr, Tübingen, 1960), p. 416.

16 Ibid., p. 323.

17 Rommetveit, 1974, 119.

18 Sextus Empiricus, *Outlines of Pyrrhonism* (London, Heinemann, 1955 [c.150]), p. 179.

19 Alain Badiou, *Ethics: An Essay on the Understanding of Evil* (London, Verso, 2001), p. 136.

20 Michael Tye, *Consciousness, Color and Content* (Cambridge, Massachusetts, MIT Press, 2000), p. 48 (my italics).

21 Ibid., p. 49.

22 David Wiggins, 'On Singling out an Object Determinately,' in *Subject, Thought and Context*, eds. Philip Pettit and John MacDowell (Oxford, Clarendon Press, 1986), pp. 169–80.

23 Ibid., p. 175.

24 Slavoj Žižek, *The Ticklish Subject: The Absent Centre of Political Ontology* (London, Verso, 1999), pp. 104–7; *The Fragile Absolute*, pp. 148 (see note 1).

25 Immanuel Kant, *Critique of Practical Reason* (New York, Macmillan 1956 [1788]), pp. 152–3.

26 Žižek, *The Ticklish Subject*, p. 25 (see note 23).

27 Žižek, *The Fragile Absolute*, p. 145.

28 Žižek, *The Ticklish Subject*, p. 211.

29 Sir Alan Gardiner, 'De Saussure's Analysis of the *signe linguistique*,' *Acta Linguistica*, 4 (1944), 104–110 (p. 109).

30 Alexander Bryan Johnson, *A Treatise on Language*, ed. David Rynin (New York, Dover Publications, 1968), p. 100.

31 Žižek, *The Fragile Absolute*, p. 115.

32 Edmond Wright, 'Sociology and the Irony Model,' *Sociology*, 12:5 (1978), 523–43 pp. 528–40). p. 28.

33 Žižek, *The Fragile Absolute*, p. 28.

34 Roy Wood Sellars, 'The Epistemology of Evolutionary Naturalism,' *Mind*, 28:112 (1919), 407–26 (p. 407).

35 Žižek, *The Ticklish Subject*, p. 272.

36   Žižek, *Did Somebody say Totalitarianism? Five Interventions in the (Mis)use of a Notion* (London, Verso, 2001), p. 28.
37   Slavoj Žižek, *The Sublime Object of Ideology* (London, Verso, 1989), pp. 27–8.
38   Vološinov, p. 176 (see note 4).
39   Ernst Cassirer, *An Essay on Man: An Introduction to the Philosophy of Human Culture* (New Haven and London, Yale University Press, 1944), p. 83.
40   Jean Baudrillard, *Selected Writings*, ed. Mark Poster (Cambridge, Polity Press, 1988), p. 169.
41   Don Cupitt, *Taking Leave of God* (London, SCM Press, 1980).
42   Žižek, *The Ticklish Subject*, p. 267.
43   Ibid., p. 342–3.
44   Žižek, *The Sublime Object of Ideology*, pp. 36–49 (see note 36).

Chance and Repetition in Kieslowski's Films

Dedicated to the memory of Elizabeth Wright

Krzysztof Kieslowski's interest in the role of chance in determining the multiple possible outcomes of a dramatic situation (exemplarily in his *Blind Chance*, but also in *Veronique* and *Red*), offers yet another example of the well-known phenomenon of the old artistic forms pushing against their own boundaries by way of mobilizing procedures which, at least from our retroactive view, seem to point towards a new technology that will be able to serve as a more 'natural' and appropriate 'objective correlative' to the life-experience the old forms endeavoured to render with their excessive experimentations.[1] It can thus be claimed that a whole series of narrative procedures in nineteenth-century novels announce not only the standard narrative cinema (recall the intricate use of 'flashback' in Emily Brontë or of 'cross-cutting' and 'close-ups' in Dickens), but sometimes even the modernist cinema (recall the use of 'off-space' in *Madame Bovary*) — as if a new perception of life was already here, but was still struggling to find its proper means of articulation, until it finally found it in cinema.

It can be claimed that today, we are approaching a homologous threshold: a new 'life experience' is in the air, a perception of life that explodes the form of the linear-centred narrative and renders life as a multiform flow; up to the domain of the 'hard' sciences (quantum physics and its Multiple-Reality interpretation; neo-Darwinism) we seem to be haunted by the chanciness of life and the alternate versions of reality — to quote Stephen Jay Gould's blunt formulation which uses precisely the cinema metaphor: 'Wind back the film of life and play it again. The history of evolution will be totally different'.[2]

Either life is experienced as a series of multiple parallel destinies that interact and are crucially affected by meaningless contingent encounters, the points at which one series intersects with and intervenes into another (see Altman's *Shortcuts*), or different versions/outcomes of the same plot are repeatedly enacted (the 'parallel universes' or 'alternative possible worlds' scenarios — even 'serious' historians themselves recently produced a volume of *Virtual Histories*, reading crucial events, from Cromwell's victory over the Stuarts and the American War of Independence to the disintegration of Communism, as hinging on unpredictable and sometimes even improbable chances). These perceptions of our reality as one of the possible, often even not the most probable, outcomes of an 'open' situation, this notion that other possible outcomes are not simply cancelled out but continue to haunt our 'true' reality as a spectre of what might have happened, conferring on our reality the status of extreme fragility and contingency, implicitly clash with the predominant 'linear' narrative forms of our literature and cinema — they seem to call for a new artistic medium in which they would not be an eccentric excess, but its 'proper' mode of functioning. One can argue that the cyberspace hypertext is such a new medium in which this life experience will find its 'natural,' more appropriate objective correlative,[3] and that Kieslowski's seemingly 'obscurantist' dealing with the topic of the role of chance and of parallel alternative histories is to be perceived as yet another endeavour to articulate the new life experience in the old cinematic medium that promotes linear narrative. We find in Kieslowski three versions of alternative histories: direct presentation of three possible outcomes in *Blind Chance*, the presentation of two outcomes through the theme of the double in *The Double Life of Veronique*, and the presentation of two outcomes through the 'flashback in present' in *Red*. What interests Kieslowski in the motif of alternative histories is the notion of *ethical choice*, ultimately the choice between 'calm life' and 'mission'.

Is, however, this awareness of multiple universes really as liberating as it appears? The (false) ordinary perception that we live in one 'true' reality, far from containing us to a closed universe, relieves us from the unbearable awareness of the multitude of alternate universes which envelop us. That is to say, the fact that there is only one reality leaves the space open for other possibilities, i.e. for a choice: it might have been different. If, however, these different possibilities are all in a way realized, we get a claustrophobic universe in which there is no freedom of choice precisely because ALL choices are already realized. Perhaps, it is the horrifying awareness of this absolute closure that is expressed by the desperate cry that opens *Blind Chance*. Here is the film's storyline: Witek runs after a train. Three variations follow on how such a seemingly banal incident could influence the rest of his life. One: he catches the train, meets an honest Communist and himself becomes a Party activist. Two: while running for the train he bumps into a railway guard, is arrested, brought to trial and sent to unpaid labour in a park where he meets someone from the opposition. He, in turn, becomes a militant dissident. Three: he simply misses the train, returns to his interrupted studies, marries a fellow student and leads a peaceful life as a doctor unwilling to get mixed up in politics. He is sent abroad to a symposium; in mid-air the plane he is on explodes.

How do these three alternative narrative lines relate to each other? The film opens with the 'primal scream' shot: a terrified male face looks into the camera and utters a cry of pure horror — is this not Witek moments before his death, while the plane which was to take him to a medical symposium in the West is crashing minutes after its take off from the Warsaw airport (we learn this in the last shot of the film, at the end of the *third* narrative)? Is, then, the entire film not the flashback of a person who, aware that he is close to his death, quickly runs not only through his life (as is usually reported that people do when they know they will die shortly), but through his THREE possible lives? The scream that opens the film — the desperate 'Nooo!' of Witek falling down to his certain death — is thus the zero level exempted from the three virtual universes. One is tempted to follow here the hypothesis[4] according to which these three alternative versions are intertwined, so that the hero escapes from each one into the next one: the deadlock of the socialist apparatchik's career pushes him into dissidence, and the non-satisfaction with dissidence into private profession. Each version involves a reflexive stance towards the previous one, like the second Veronique who seems to be aware of the experience of the first one. It is only the third version which is 'real': just before dying, Witek runs through the two alternative life-stories in which he would not die ('what would have happened if I were to catch the train; if, while running for it, I were to hit a policeman. . .'), but they both end up in a deadlock which pushes him to the next story.

Tom Tykwer's *Run, Lola, Run* (Germany, 1998) is a kind of postmodern frenetic remake of *Blind Chance*. Lola, a Berlin punk girl (Franka Potente), has 20 minutes to collect by any means 100.000 German Marks to save her boyfriend from certain death, and what follows are the three alternate outcomes. (1) her boyfriends gets killed; (2) she gets killed; (3) she succeeds, AND her boyfriend finds the lost money, so they end up happy together with the 100.000 DM profit. Here, also, a whole series of features signals that not only the heroine, but even other people somehow mysteriously remember what happened in the preceding version(s). Although, in its tone (the frenetic, adrenalin-charged pace, life-asserting energy, the happy end), *Lola* is the very opposite of *Blind Chance*, the formal matrix is the same: in both cases, one can interpret the film as if only the third story is the 'real' one, the other two staging the fantasmatic price the subject has to pay for the 'real' outcome.

The interest of *Lola* resides in its tonality: not only in the fast rhythm, the rapid-fire montage, the use of stills (frozen images), the pulsating exuberance and vitality of the heroine, but, above all, in the way these visual features are embedded in the soundtrack — the constant, uninterrupted, techno-music soundscape whose rhythm renders Lola's — and, by extension, ours, the spectators' — heartbeat. One should always bear in mind that, notwithstanding all the dazzling visual brilliance of the film, its images are subordinated to the musical soundscape, to its frenetic compulsive rhythm which goes on forever and cannot be suspended even for a minute — it can only explode in an outburst of exuberant vitality, in the guise of Lola's uninhibited scream which occurs in each of the three versions of the story. This is why a film like *Lola* can only appear against the background of the Music TV-channel culture. One could accomplish here the same reversal Fredric Jameson proposed apropos Hemingway's style: it is not that *Lola*'s formal properties adequately express the narrative; it is rather that the film's narrative itself was invented in order to be able to practise the style. The first words of the film ('the game lasts 90 minutes, everything else is just theory') provide the proper co-ordinates of a video game: as in the usual survival video game, Lola is given three lives. 'Real life' itself is thus rendered as a fictional video-game experience — and what one should resist here is precisely the temptation to oppose *Lola* and Kieslowski's *Blind Chance* along the lines of the opposition between low and high culture (Tykwer's video games techno rock MTV universe versus Kieslowski's existential pondering stance). Although this is in a way true — or, rather, a truism, the more important point is that *Lola* is much more adequate to the basic matrix of alternative spins of the narrative: it is *Blind Chance* which ultimately appears clumsy, artificial, as if the film tries to tell its story in an inadequate form, while *Lola*'s form perfectly fits its narrative content.[5]

Kieslowski himself alludes to the virtualization of reality in his claim that '[t]he theme of *Red* is in the conditional mood. (. . .) what would have happened if the Judge had been born forty years later. (. . .) It would be lovely if we could go back to the age of twenty. How many better, wiser things we could have done! But it's impossible. That's why I made this film — that maybe life can be lived better than we do'.[6] The theme of the 'double life' clearly resonates not only in *Red*, but also in *Blue* and *White*: in *Blue*, Julie desperately endeavours to (re)create an alternative life after the traumatic accident, while in *White*, Karol tries to reinvent a new career and life after his humiliating reduction to a social drop-out. There are traces of the alternate reality approach even in *Decalogue* 4, which was planned initially as three variations, on the model of *Blind Chance* (the father's story; the daughter's story; what really happened); Kieslowski wisely adopted a more complex procedure in which the three stories coexist in a kind of palimpsest: 'the variants are not successive (as in *Blind Chance* or *The Double Life of Veronique*), but present themselves simultaneously through the work's self-referential meditation on acting'.[7] The 'same' narrative shifts between different fantasmatic supports: sometimes, Anka acts as if there are no obstacles to her incestuous fantasy; at other times, father acts as if he and Anka are of the same age; at yet other times, the oppressive social reality makes itself felt.

Red presents us with a unique case of 'contemporary flashback': the Judge's alternate *past*, his missed opportunity, is staged as the *present* of another person (Auguste) — Auguste's predicament is the exact repetition of the Judge's predicament thirty years before. Auguste and the Judge are thus not two persons, but two versions of one and the same person — no wonder they never meet, since this meeting would function as the uncanny encounter of a double. The parallels in their respective lives are numerous: the Judge, like Auguste, was betrayed by a blonde woman two years older than him; his book also fell open to a particular page the night before his exam, where he was asked the very question answered on that page. No wonder, then, that the Judge says to Valentine: 'Maybe you're the woman I never met' — meeting her decades ago would save him the way Valentine will NOW save Auguste. One should approach in the same way *The Double Life of Veronique*: the image of two Veroniques should not deceive us — as the title says, we have the double life of (one) Veronique, i.e. the same person is allowed to redeem (or lose?) herself by being given another chance and repeating the fatal choice. All the mystique of being spiritually connected with another being is thoroughly misplaced.

The idea of the time-space continuum (time as the fourth dimension of space) in modern physics means, among other things, that a certain event (the encounter of multiple particles) can be much more elegantly and convincingly explained if we posit that only one particle travels forward and backward in time. Let's take Richard Feynmann's classic space-time diagram of the collision between *two* photons in a certain point of time: this collision produces an electron-positron pair, each of the two going its separate way. The positron then meets another electron; they annihilate each other and create again *two* photons which depart in the opposite direction. What Feynmann proposes is that, if we introduce the space-time continuum, i.e. the notion of time as the fourth dimension of space which can also be traversed in two directions, forward and backwards, we can explain the same process in a much simpler way: there is ONLY ONE particle, an electron, which emits two photons; this causes it to reverse its direction in time. Travelling backward in time as a positron, it absorbs two photons, thus becomes an electron again and reverses its direction in time, again moving forward. This logic involves the static space-time picture described by Einstein: events do not unfold with the flow of time, but present themselves complete, and in this total picture, movements backward and forward in time are as usual as movements backward and forward in space. The illusion that there is a 'flow' of time results from our narrow awareness which allows us to perceive only a part of the total space-time continuum.[8] And is not something similar going on in the alternative narratives? Beneath ordinary reality, there is another shadowy pre-ontological realm of virtualities in which the same person travels forth and back, 'testing' different scenarios: Veronique-electron crashes (dies), then travels back in time and does it again, this time surviving.

In *Veronique*, we are thus not dealing with the 'mystery' of the communication of two Veroniques, but with the ONE AND THE SAME Veronique who travels back and forth in time. For that reason, the key scene of the film is the encounter of the two Veroniques in the large square in which a Solidarity political demonstration is taking place: this encounter is rendered in a vertiginous circular shot reminiscent of the famous 360 degrees shot from Hitchcock's *Vertigo*; afterwards, when the French Veronique is introduced, it becomes clear that the perplexity of the Polish Weronika at this moment resulted from her obscure awareness that she was about to have an impossible encounter with her double (later, we see her photo taken at that moment by the French Veronique).[9] Consequently, is this camera's circular movement not to be read as signalling the danger of the 'end of the world,' somehow like the standard scene of the science-fiction films about alternative realities, in which the passage from one to another universe takes the shape of a terrifying primordial vortex threatening to swallow all consistent reality? The camera's circular movement thus signals that we are on the verge of the vortex in which different realities mix, that this vortex is already exerting its influence: if we make one step further — that is to say, if the two

Veronique's were actually to confront and recognize each other — , reality would disintegrate, because such an encounter of a person with her own double, with *herself* in another time-space dimension, is precluded by the very fundamental structure of the universe.

This encounter has a different meaning for each of the two Veroniques: for the Polish Weronika, it marks, in the traditional Romantic mode, the encounter of death (and, effectively, soon after she dies), while to the French Veronique, the awareness that there is her double clearly confronts her with the possibility of choice — she may have chosen a different life (the singing career), which, again, would have lead to her death. This is the reason why the double causes such anxiety: the double IS directly the object that the subject refuses to be. In Wolfgang Petersen's thriller *Shattered* (1991), Tom Berenger barely survives a car accident: when, weeks later, he awakens in the hospital, with his face and body patched up by plastic surgery, he has total amnesia concerning his identity — he cannot remember who he is, although all the people around him, including a woman who claims to be his wife (Greta Scacchi), treat him as the head of a rich corporation. After a series of mysterious events, he goes to an abandoned warehouse where he was told that, in a barrel full of oil, the corpse of the person he had killed is hidden. When he pulls the body's head out of the liquid, he stiffens in consternation — the head is HIS OWN. (The solution to the mystery: he is effectively not the husband, but the lover of the woman who claims to be his wife. When he barely survived the accident while driving the husband's car, with his face disfigured beyond recognition, the wife killed her husband, identified HIM as her husband and ordered the surgeons to reconstruct his face on the model of her husband's.) This horror of encountering oneself in the guise of one's double, outside oneself, is the ultimate truth of the subject's self-identity: in it, the subject encounters itself as an object.

Recall Humbert Humbert from Nabokov's *Lolita*: in a stroke of genius, Nabokov made his Christian name coincide with his father's name — there is already the structure of the double in his very name! (And, in a gesture of supreme Nabokovian irony, Kieslowski named the hero of *White* Karol Karol.) Humbert Humbert thus *needs* Quilty, his obscene double who persecutes the couple of him and Lolita: Quilty is the paranoiac return in the Real of the paternal Name foreclosed from the Symbolic (as is signalled by Humbert Humbert's name, where the proper family name is missing). This is how *Lolita* signals the impossibility of sexual relationship: the liaison of Humbert Humbert and Lolita is simultaneously hindered and sustained by the intervention of a paranoiac Third — although fanatically opposed to psychoanalysis, Nabokov was well aware of the link between the suspension of the paternal function and the murderous paranoiac relationship with one's double.[10] Consequently, it is wrong to read *Lolita* in a vulgar pseudo-Freudian way, as a case of 'repressed homosexuality': the point is not that Humbert Humbert chooses a nymphet in order to avoid the direct homosexual engagement with his double Quilty — on the contrary, Quilty is the necessary Third who supplements Humbert's impossible relationship with Lolita. — And the same goes for the two Veroniques. In the passage from the Polish Weronika to the French Veronique, after Weronika dies on the concert stage, we get the Dreyeresque shot from the grave (the impossible point-of-view shot of her corpse), which is then followed by the direct cut to Veronique making love and inexplicably feeling sad, as if she sensed some unknown loss — the trace of her double interferes as the *Liebesstoerer*, the intruder who disturbs the harmony of the sexual act. Again, the figure of the double is strictly correlative to the impossibility of sexual relationship.

So what is this impossibility? In Cuba, when one man boasts to another 'I HAD that woman!,' he implies not just 'straight' vaginal intercourse, but anal penetration — 'straight' intercourse is still considered a form of petting, of foreplay, and it is only the anal penetration that stands for the fully consummated sexual relation. Why is it so? Because the vagina is considered a pale, distorted copy of the anal opening: the anus is somehow like the pure Platonic Idea (a clear and simple round hole, with no hair or crevices), while the vagina is its distorted material realization, full of protuberances and outgrowths, far from the ideal simplicity of the anus. Is this not yet another way to supplement the non-existence of the sexual relationship — the 'natural' penetration is devalued as secondary in relation to its 'unnatural' ideal model? The male counterpoint to it is the difference phallus/penis, as it is mobilized in the standard porno shot of a woman being penetrated anally and at the same time displaying the hole of her spread vagina — as if to say 'Although I am penetrated by the *penis*, the hole is still open for *phallus*' ... Some Hindu priests allegedly can do impossible things with their penises: not only fully controlling erection with their will; not only knowing how to ejaculate inside instead of outside, so that, instead of being released and spilled out, lost outside, the energy of orgasm gets back into the body and thus contributes to a heightened spiritual energy;

they are even are able to suck small amounts of liquid like milk with their penises. . . The fascination of these cases resides in the fact that these priests seem to overcome the exceptional status of the penis, the independence of its erection of the subject's will — in short, in their unique case, penis and phallus DO coincide.

Each of the three men in Neil LaBute's *Our Friends and Neighbours* is caught in his solipsistic fantasmatic space: the first one, the only decent 'good guy,' can only find proper satisfaction in masturbation, and cannot satisfy his wife; the second one, the drama teacher, is a sleazy fast-talking seducer who alienates his wife by talking all the time during the sexual act, communicating his (private, not shared) fantasies and thus spoiling the act by rendering public its fantasmatic support — in the middle of the act, the wife cruelly tells him to shut up and go on fucking; the third one, a cold, sadistic manipulator, engages in 'hot talk' allegedly addressed to the feminine partner during the sexual act, while he effectively practises intensive body-building training. Their feminine partners are also frustrated (the teacher's wife, tired of talking, engages in a lesbian relationship: the disappointed 'good' guy's wife searches for a lover among the other two men). The film is profoundly theological, pervaded by a bleak vision of a dark 'godless' universe in which the solipsistic search for pleasure unavoidably ends in utter failure and despair (LaBute is a practising Mormon). All the characters are caught in a mechanic web of relations, like the puppets in some late-eighteenth-century French aristocratic chamber comedy of manners — exemplary here is the scene in the art gallery where five times different visitors ask the Nastassja Kinski character the same predictable set of questions and get the same answers ('Is this piece part of a series or does it stand alone?,' 'Are you the artist?,' etc.)

However, one should not dismiss these frustrations as the result of a specific historical situation; a more radical deadlock lurks beneath them. In a TV movie about the global ecological catastrophe, the wife rejects her husband's love-making — her reproach to him is that he is doing it to her 'as if you want to make a statement' with it. This formulation renders succinctly what Lacan has in mind with his thesis that there is no sexual relationship: the sexual act is not possible in the mode of 'making a statement,' as a symbolic assertion. Recall the first great Wagnerian love dialogue, that of the Dutchman and Senta from *The Flying Dutchman*: the two lovers seem to ignore each other's physical presence, they do not even look each other face to face, they simply engage each in his/her intimate fantasmatic vision of the other. 'There is no sexual relationship' means (among other things) that, during a 'straight' intercourse, the man *qua* obsessional thinks of *another* woman, the true addressee of his passionate whispers, reducing the woman he holds in his hands to the material support of the fantasmatic *objet petit a*: in an inverse way, the woman *qua* hysteric doesn't want to be the object-cause of her man's (other's) desire, so she imagines some other woman, not her, in bed with her partner, while she is 'somewhere else'. What, however, if these two fantasies *overlap*, so that, during the intercourse, the other woman — the woman who the 'actual' woman engaged in the sexual act fantasizes as the one who is in bed with her partner — is the very woman the male partner imagines in bed with him? Suppose we have a woman and a man engaged in 'straight' sex — what, however, if they are only able to do it because he secretly identifies with a lesbian woman and she IS a lesbian, so that, at the fantasmatic level, the act is effectively that of a lesbian couple doing it with a dildo? The fantasmatic support of a 'straight' sexual relationship is never the scenario of a 'straight sex,' but always a mixture of 'perverse' elements. Maybe, therein resides the only possible 'harmony' in sex — Lacan himself says somewhere that sexual relation can work if man's and woman's fantasies overlap.

The feminine fantasy of being someone else in the relation with her husband also accounts for what, perhaps, is the ultimate melodramatic scenario, detectable from Rudolph Mate's *No Sad Songs for Me* to *Stepmom*: the idea of a woman who, dying of cancer or some other mortal disease, in her last weeks organizes things so that, after her death, a new, younger woman will replace her as the new partner of her husband and the new mother to her children. (The title of one of the TV-movies in this series is indicative: *When I am no longer there* — does this not provide the most succinct formula of the fantasy gaze, i.e. of the subject erasing herself out of the picture, remaining only as the pure disembodied spectral gaze observing the idyll that emerges in her absence?) This is the paradigmatically feminine fantasy of obliterating the inexistence of sexual relationship: if she erases herself out of the picture, the new relationship of her husband will be a full one. As Joan Copjec convincingly demonstrated, this same basic fantasmatic matrix is at work in *Stella Dallas*: Barbara Stanwyck does not sacrifice herself for her daughter; she rather 'erases herself out of the picture' in order to be able to assume the position of a pure gaze witnessing through the window-frame (of fantasy) the newly established perfect family of her daughter and her new ideal parental couple, her father and his new appropriate wife.[11] This fantasy of the feminine self-withdrawal, self-erasure from the picture, finds its ultimate expression in Richard Strauss's *Der Rosenkavalier*, in the words of the Marschallin which open the final trio: 'I chose to love him in the right way, so that I would love even his love for another!'

Something similar happens in Goethe's *Elective Affinities* where, during the sexual intercourse between wife and husband, each of them fantasizes about embracing another partner he/she is really in love with (the husband Ottilie, the wife Hauptmann) — what we thus obtain is the paradox of *marital fidelity in the guise of double unfaithfulness*. This ideal-impossible, purely fantasmatic couple of Hauptmann and Ottilie is nonetheless not without material incidence: the child born from this act of marital copulation *qua* double treachery gives body to this impossible couple, i.e. he has the hair and face of Ottilie and the eyes of Hauptmann, and thus renders visible the illicit desire of both husband and wife — no wonder that he dies soon after his birth.

And, perhaps, this possibility of overlapping fantasies is what sustains the subtle literary figure of the 'vanishing mediator' who brings together a couple by intentionally mistranslating their messages to each other. In a story by Guy de Maupassant, pupils in a class who have a shy teacher, intend to play a cruel joke on him by arranging for a date between him and the poor cleaning woman of the school — they tell each of the two the invented story of how the other confided in them that he/she has a concealed love interest in him/her. Hidden under the roof, they then observe the encounter, expecting a good laugh after the couple are embarrassed by discovering that they were victims of a cruel practical joke. However, when they finally meet, the couple gently establishes contact, (falsely) assured of the other's sympathy, and they end up happily married. In all these cases, a double lie results in a final harmony.

This hysterical rejection of being the body that one has is today clearly discernible in the two opposed stances with regard to woman's body: in late-liberal promiscuous tolerance, women freely expose themselves as part of the capitalist universalized prostitution, while religious fundamentalism forces women to wear veils, so that nothing is visible of them but their two eyes. This oscillation itself is significant: crucial to this is the structural ambiguity as to its meaning — on the one hand, one can say that the covered woman designates the victim of extreme patriarchal domination, as opposed to a woman of liberal Western society free to enjoy her body; on the other hand, one can say that the Western woman is turned into the sexual object exposed to the male gaze, in contrast to the veiled woman who retains at least some dignity. The paradox, of course, is that the very fact of compelling women to be covered in order to retain their dignity asserts what it wants to deny: it automatically assumes that the view of a woman's body reduces it to an object for male sexploitation, so that the way to counteract it is not to change the nature/stance of the male gaze, but to cover its object (which, of course, in this way becomes even more fascinating). On the other hand, and in a complementary way, one can claim that, in the concrete conditions of our late capitalist society, the freedom of a woman to dispose of her body is ultimately the freedom to prostitute herself, to sell herself as on object of exchange to men. We are definitely dealing here with a kind of Hegelian 'identity of the opposites'.

Another aspect of this same tension is discernible in the cases when a gynaecologist is accused of finding sexual pleasure in touching intimate parts of his patients; the reproach here is that he did not *objectivize* his feminine patient sufficiently, that he did not treat here as effectively just an object of the medical gaze. Around the turn of the century, sexually frustrated hysterical ladies from the upper-class families regularly visited doctors who applied a hand-massage on their genitals in order to relieve them of their pathological tension and unrest — to masturbate a feminine patient was considered a painful and delicate medical duty, not a perversion. This is the reason why doctors welcomed the invention of (electric and mechanic) machines to 'massage' the feminine genitalia (what today we call vibrators): these machines were not considered sex toys, but medical instruments. Does this strange example not tell us a lot about the shifts in the discursive formation of sexuality, i.e. about how a certain form of sexual (dis)satisfaction was depersonalized-objectivized, reduced to a pathological tension to be appeased through the doctor's intervention? The enigma here is: did all of them, doctors and patients, just feign and play an obscene game, being well aware that it is all about sexual (dis)satisfaction, or did they effectively treat the dissatisfaction as an objectivized illness ('hysterical tension') to be properly treated (by the masturbatory massage)? Perhaps, it effectively WAS possible to 'desubjectivize' sexual dissatisfaction into an objective affliction?

So, for Lacan, 'there is no sexual relationship' because there are always *at least three* in it, never just the two (if they are two) engaged partners — and *this* is what complicates the issue of homosexuality: it is never just the relationship between the two persons, so the true enigma is *who is the fantasized Third*. In a lesbian relationship, this third could well be a paternal phallic figure (which is why 'lesbian phallus' is a pertinent category). The need for this fantasmatic third arises from the excess which escapes the (sexual) partner's grasp: on the women's side, it is the feminine Mystery beneath the provocative masquerade, forever eluding the male grasp; on the male side, it is the drive which makes him stick unconditionally to his (political, artistic, religious, professional) Vocation. The eternal male paranoia is that the woman is jealous of this part of him which resists her seductive charm, and that she wants to snatch it from him, to induce him to sacrifice that kernel of his creativity for her (afterwards, of course, she will drop him, because her interest for him was sustained precisely by that mysterious ingredient which resisted her grasp). This aspect accounts for the popularity of Colleen McCullough's *Thornbirds* in which Father Ralph is torn between his love for Maggie and his unconditional religious vocation — paradoxically, a chaste priest is one of the emblematic figures of the non-castrated Other, of the Other not bound by the symbolic Law.

Lacan provided the ultimate formulation of this impossibility in his 'formulas of sexuation': the masculine side combines universality with its constitutive exception, while the feminine side asserts the non-All as the paradoxical obverse of the lack of exception.[12] One should read the two levels that define each position as 'appearance versus truth': the upper level provides the 'appearance,' while the lower level discloses its 'truth'. The 'appearance' of the masculine position is that of universality, while its 'truth' is the constitutive exception/transgression (say, the Hero-Master who violates the law in order to constitute it); the 'appearance' of the feminine position is the mysterious Exception, the Feminine which resists the universal symbolic order, while its 'truth' is that *there is nothing outside* the symbolic order, no exception. If, then, the masculine stance is that of the law-suspending exceptional violence of the Master concealed behind the Universality, i.e. the Exception that grounds the Universality, the feminine stance designates the hysterical split — a woman focuses on something 'in her more than herself,' her narcissistic secret treasure that escapes the male Master's universal grasp, and the truth of it is that *there is no secret*, that femininity is a masquerade concealing nothing (as was clear to Otto Weininger, who equated femininity with the ontological Nothingness). The standard opposition of the masculine subject fully integrated into the symbolic law and the feminine subject partially resisting it is thus thoroughly misleading: it is the masculine position which involves the Exception, while in the feminine position, there is nothing that is *not* inscribed into the 'phallic' symbolic function.

So, to conclude, Kieslowski's universe of alternate realities is thoroughly ambiguous. On the one hand, its lesson seems to be that we live in the world of alternate realities in which, as in a cyberspace game, when one choice leads to the catastrophic ending, we can return to the starting point and make another, better, choice — what was the first time a suicidal mistake, can the second time be done in a correct way, so that the opportunity is not missed. In *The Double Life of Veronique*, Veronique learns from Weronika, avoids the suicidal choice of singing and survives; in *Red*, Auguste avoids the mistake of the Judge; even *White* ends with the prospect of Karol and his French bride getting a second chance and remarrying. The very title of Annette Insdorf's recent book on Kieslowski, *Double Lives, Second Chances*, points in this direction: the other life is here to give us a second chance, i.e. 'repetition becomes accumulation, with a prior mistake as a base for successful action'.[13] However, while it sustains the prospect of repeating the passed choices and thus retrieving the missed opportunities, this universe can also be interpreted in the opposite, much darker, way. There is a material feature of Kieslowski's films which long ago attracted the attention of some perspicuous critics; suffice it to recall the use of filters in *A Short Film About Killing*:

> The city and its surroundings are shown in a specific way. The lighting cameraman on this film, Slawek Idziak, used filters which he'd made specially. Green filters so that the colour in the film is specifically greenish. Green is supposed to be the colour of spring, the colour of hope, but if you put a green filter on the camera, the world becomes much crueller, duller and emptier.[14]

Furthermore, in *A Short Film About Killing*, the filters are used 'as a kind of mask, darkening parts of the image which Kieslowski and Idziak did not wish to show'.[15] This procedure of having 'large chunks smogged out'[16] — not as part of the formulaic depiction of a dream or a vision, but in shots rendering the gray everyday reality — directly evokes the Gnostic notion of the universe which was created imperfect and is as such not yet fully constituted. The closest one can get to it in reality is, perhaps, the countryside in extreme places like Iceland or the Land of Fire at the utmost south of Latin America: patches of grass and wild hedges are intersected by the barren raw earth or gravel with cracks out of which sulphuric steam and fire gush out, as if the pre-ontological primordial Chaos is still able to penetrate the cracks of the imperfectly constituted/formed reality.

Kieslowski's universe is a Gnostic universe, a not-yet-fully consti-tuted universe created by a perverse and confused, idiotic God who screwed up the work of Creation, producing an imperfect world, and then trying to save whatever can be saved by repeated new attempts—we are all 'Children of a Lesser God'.[17] In the main-stream Hollywood itself, this uncanny in-between dimension is clearly discernible in what is arguably the most effective scene in *Alien 4: Resurrection*: the cloned Ripley (Sigourney Weaver) enters the labora-tory room in which the previous seven aborted attempts to clone her are on display—here she encounters the ontologically failed, defective versions of herself, up to the almost successful version with her own face, but with some of her limbs distorted so that they resemble the limbs of the Alien Thing—this creature asks Ripley to kill her, and, in an outburst of violent rage, Ripley effectively destroys the entire horror-exhibition.—This idea of multiple imperfect universes can be discerned at two levels in Kieslowski's opus: (1) the botched character of reality as depicted in his films, and the ensuing repeated attempts to (re)create a new, better, reality; (2) with regard to Kieslowski himself as author, we also have the repeated attempts to tell the same story in a slightly different way (not only the difference between TV and movie version of *Decalogue* 5 and 6, but also his idea of making twenty different versions of *Veronique* and playing them in different theatres in Paris—a different version for each theatre). In this eternally repeated rewriting, the 'quilting point' is forever missing: there never is a final version, the work is never done and actually put in circulation, delivered from the author to the big Other of the Public. (Is the recent fashion of the later release of the allegedly more authentic 'director's cut' also not part of the same economy?) What does this absence of the 'final version' MEAN—this everlasting deferral of the moment when, like God after his six days work, the author can say 'It's done!' and take a rest?

The 'virtualization' of our life-experience, the explosion/de-hiscence of the single 'true' reality into the multitude of parallel lives, is strictly correlative to the assertion of the proto-cosmic abyss of chaotic, ontologically not yet fully constituted reality—this primordial, pre-symbolic, inchoate 'stuff' is the very neutral medium in which the multitude of parallel universes can coexist. In contrast to the standard notion of one fully determined and ontologically constituted reality, with regard to which all other realities are its secondary shadows, copies, reflections, 'reality' itself is thus multiplied into the spectral plurality of virtual realities, beneath which lurks the pre-ontological proto-reality, the Real of the unformed ghastly matter. The first clearly to articulate this pre-ontological dimension was F.W.J. Schelling with his notion of the unfathomable Ground of God, something in God that is not-yet-God, not yet the fully constituted reality.[18]

SLAVOJ ŽIŽEK
Kulturwissenschaftliches Institut, Essen

NOTES

1   For a more detailed exploration of this phenomenon, see Slavoj Žižek, *The Art of the Ridiculous Sublime* (Seattle, Washington University Press, 2000).

2   Stephen Jay Gould, 'Time Scales and the Year 2000,' in Umberto Eco, Stephen Jay Gould, Henri Carriere, and Jean Delumeau, *Conversations About the End of Time* (Harmondsworth, Penguin Books, 2000), p. 41.

3   See Janet Murray, *Hamlet on the Holodeck* (Cambridge, Massachusetts, MIT Press, 1997), pp. 37–8.

4   Of Alain Masson, in *Krzystof Kieslowski. Textes reunis et presentes par Vincent Amiel* (Paris, Positif, 1997), p. 57.

5   It is nonetheless interesting to know that, in the Fall of 2000, Tom Tykwer was making *Heaven*, a film based on the scenario co-written by Kieslowski and Piesiewicz, the first part of the planned trilogy *Heaven, Hell, Purgatory* — so there *is* some affinity between the two directors.

6   Insdorf (see Annette Insdorf, *Double Lives, Second Chances*, New York, Miramax Books, 1999, p. 175) claims that in this conversation Kieslowski directly referred to Kierkegaard's *Repetition*.

7   Paul Coates, 'The curse of the law: *The Decalogue*,' in *Lucid Dreams: The Films of Krzysztof Kieslowski*, ed. by Paul Coates (Trowbridge, Flick Books, 1999), p. 103.

8   See Gary Zukav, *The Dancing Wu Li Masters* (London, Fontana, 1979), pp. 237–238.

9   Vincent Amiel, *Kieslowski* (Paris, Rivages, 1995), p. 42–4.

10 More precisely, the displacement of this impossibility is triple: Charlotte loves Humbert Humbert who loves Lolita who loves Quilty who doesn't love anyone.

11 See Joan Copjec, 'Introduction,' in Joan Copjec, ed., *Shades of Noir* (London, Verso, 1993).

12 On these 'formulas of sexuation,' see Jacques Lacan, *Encore* (New York, Norton, 1998).

13 See Annette Insdorf, op.cit., p. 165.

14 *Kieslowski on Kieslowski*, ed. Danusia Stok (London, Faber and Faber 1993), p. 161.

15 Charles Eidsvik, '*Decalogues* 5 and 6 and the two *Short Films,*' in *Lucid Dreams*, p. 85 (see note 7).

16 Ibid.

17 See Vincent Amiel, *Kieslowski*, p. 64/70.

18 And the ultimate irony is that this same point holds for Schelling's writing itself, for the very text(s) in which he deployed this pre-ontological dimension of proto-reality, his *Weltalter* fragment: there are three consecutive drafts, as if we have the three alternative-reality versions of the same text. See Chapter I of Slavoj Žižek, *The Indivisible Remainder* (London, Verso Books, 1996).

Enjoy!

A review of Slavoj Žižek's *The Indivisible Remainder, The Abyss of Freedom/Ages of the World, The Plague of Fantasies, and The Ticklish Subject*[1]

Schopenhauer saw us all as permanently pregnant with monsters, bearing at the very core of our being something implacably alien to it. He called this the Will, which was the stuff out of which we were made and yet was utterly indifferent to us, lending us an illusion of purpose but itself aimless and senseless. Freud, who was much taken with Schopenhauer, offered us a non-metaphysical version of this monstrosity in the notion of desire, a profoundly inhuman process which is deaf to meaning, which has its own sweet way with us and secretly cares for nothing but itself. Desire is nothing personal; it is an affliction what was lying in wait for us from the outset, a perversion in which we were plunged at birth. For Freud, what makes us human subjects is this foreign body lodged inside us, which invades our flesh like a lethal virus and yet, like the Almighty for Thomas Aquinas, is closer to us than we are to ourselves.

This 'Thing,' as the psychoanalyst Jacques Lacan calls it, with horror movies in mind, is otherwise known as the Real, in the Lacanian Holy Trinity of the Real, the Imaginary and the Symbolic. It is also the chief protagonist of the work of the Slovenian philosopher Slavoj Žižek, who by drawing our attention to this most underprivileged of Lacan's three categories, challenges his fashionable image as a 'post-structuralist' thinker. Žižek's Lacan is not the philosopher of the floating signifier but a much tougher, alarming, uncanny sort of theorist altogether, who teaches that the Real which makes us what we are is not only traumatic and impenetrable but cruel, obscene, meaningless and horrifically enjoyable. Žižek himself is both dauntingly prolific and dazzlingly versatile, able to leap in a paragraph from Hegel to *Jurassic Park*, Kafka to the Ku Klux Klan; but just as Lacan's fantasy-ridden world of everyday reality conceals an immutable kernel of the Real, so Žižek's flamboyant parade of topics recircles, in book after book, to this very same subject. The almost comic versatility of his interests masks a compulsive repetition of the same. His books, as in Freud's notion of the uncanny, are both familiar and unfamiliar, breathtakingly innovative yet *dejà lu*, crammed with original insights yet perpetual recyclings of one another. If he reads

Lacan as 'a succession of attempts to seize the same traumatic kernel,' much the same can be said of his own writing, which continually bursts out anew with Schelling or Hitchcock or the war in Bosnia but never shifts its gaze from the same fearful, fascinating psychical scene.

As Žižek sees it, the Real for Lacan is almost the opposite of reality, reality being for Lacan just a low-grade place of fantasy in which we shelter from the terrors of the Real, a Soho of the psyche. The natural state of the human animal is to live a phantasmal lie. Fantasy is not the opposite of reality: it is what plugs the void in our being so that the set of fictions we call reality is able to emerge. The Real is rather like the primordial wound we incurred by our fall from the pre-Oedipal Eden, the gash in our being where we were torn loose from Nature, and from which desire flows unstaunchably. Though we repress this trauma, it persists within us as the hard core of the self. Something is missing inside us which makes us what we are, a muteness which resists being signified but which shows up negatively as the outer limit of our discourse, the point at which our representations crumble and fail.

Lacan's famous 'transcendental signifier' is just the signifier which represents this failure of representation, rather as the phallus for psychoanalysis represents the fact that it can always be cut off. The Real is what cannot be included within any of our symbolic systems, but whose very absence skews them out of shape, as a kind of vortex around which they are bent out of true. It is the factor which ensures that as human subjects we never quite add up, which throws us subtly out of kilter so that we can never be identical with ourselves. It is a version of Kant's unknowable thing-in-itself, and what is ultimately unknowable is Man himself.

The Real is desire, but for Lacan, so Žižek argues, more specifically *jouissance* or 'obscene enjoyment'. This enjoyment, which sounds rather less suburban in French, is a sublimely terrifying affair. It is the lethal pleasure of what Freud calls primary masochism, in which we reap delight from the way that the Law or superego unleashes its demented sadism on us. Enjoyment, Lacan maintains, is the only substance that psychoanalysis recognizes, and it is also Žižek's unwavering obsession. Like Schopenhauer's Will, it is a brute, self-serving affair, as devoid of meaning as the American waiter's mechanical injunction: 'Enjoy!' Like the waiter, the Law instructs us to enjoy, but does so in curiously intransitive mood: we are just to reap gratification for its own sake from the superego's crazed, pointless dictats. In *The Sublime Object of Ideology*,[2] Žižek sees ideological power as resting finally on the libidinal rather than the conceptual, on the way we hug our chains rather than the way we entertain beliefs. At the root of meaning, for both Freud and Lacan, there is always a sustaining residue of non-sense.

The Real is the 'inruption' of that non-sense into our signifying systems, and so a much crasser affair than language. But because it can never be signified, seen head-on, it is also a sort of nothing, detectable only through its effects, constructed backward after the event. We know it only from the way it acts as a drag upon discourse, as astronomers may identify a heavenly body only because of its warping effect on the space around it. For the Real to take on tangible embodiment, to crop up in the shape of voices or visions, is for us to become psychotic. The Real is the McGuffin, the joker in the pack, the sign that means nothing but itself. Every signifying system, so Žižek claims, contains a kind of super-signifier whose function is just to point to the fact that the system can't be totalized. It is that system's point of internal fracture, marking the space where it doesn't quite gel. But this absence is what organizes the whole system, and so also is a kind of presence within it. You can call this constitutive lack the human subject itself, which is necessary for any set of signs to work, yet which can never be fully encapsulated by them. But this, for Lacan, is also the function of the Real, whose very absence from consciousness is the cause of our carrying on trying to signify it there and always failing. If we failed to keep failing and trying again, if the repression was lifted and the Real burst to the surface, history would instantly cease. In this sense, the sheer impossibility of desire, the fact that we can only ever plug our lack with one poor fantasy object after another, is also what keeps us up and running. That fissure or hindrance in our being which is the Real is also what props up our identity.

This, one might claim, is a classically post-structuralist sort of doctrine. Post-structuralists have almost patented the paradox that what makes something impossible is also what makes it possible. As every English first-year student now knows, what makes a sign a sign is its difference from other signs; but this means that the difference which lends a sign its identity also makes it impossible for a sign to be complete in itself. Difference, as Jacques Derrida playfully puts it, both 'broaches and breaches' meaning. Or take the idea, much touted by Žižek, that blindness is the condition of insight, truth the upshot of misrecognition. For Nietzsche, it is only a blessed state of amnesia that enables us to act, since otherwise we would be paralysed by the nightmare of history. For Freud, we are shaped into human subjects only by a shattering repression of much that went into our making. It is this crippling forgetfulness which allows us to thrive. The roots of our conscious life must be absent from it if we are to function as subjects at all, rather as the law, if it is to maintain its august authority, must erase the fact that it was originally imposed by an arbitrary act of violence. The law cannot have been established legally, since there was no law before the law.

Žižek's favourite philosopher, after Lacan, is Hegel, who can also be used to illustrate his paradox. For Hegel, truth is not so much the opposite of error as the result of it. The cunning of Reason lies in the fact that our blunders and oversights, did we but know it, have already been reckoned into account by truth itself, as the very process by which it is achieved. Truth looks like a end-product, but turns out to encompass the whole process of trial and error which led up to it. When we are able to look back and understand that those misrecognitions were essential to the whole enterprise, this is, according to Žižek's rather heterodox view, the moment of truth or Absolute Idea. Similarly, when the analysand is able to free herself from the illusion that there is some truth quite separate from the business of transference, some transcendental knowledge of which the analyst has possession, then for the Lacanians she is *en route* to a cure. Žižek illustrates the point with the story of a man faking insanity in order to escape conscription, whose 'psychosis' takes the form of rummaging obsessively through a pile of documents saying, 'That's not it, that's not it' When the doctors, convinced by this frenetic performance, finally present him with the certificate of exemption, he exclaims, 'That's it!' What looked like the result of his behaviour was actually the cause of it, and this reversal of cause and effect is a staple of psychoanalytic theory which Žižek expounds — as he expounds everything else — with extraordinary élan.

He is, in fact, the most formidably brilliant exponent of psycho-analysis, indeed of cultural theory in general, to have emerged in Europe for decades. The fact that he hails from a former Communist society is probably not accidental in this respect, since there was always a certain market for French theory in the Eastern bloc. If the secret police do not take kindly to talk of political resistance, you can always recode it as deconstructing totalities, subverting the Master-Signifier, opening up to the Other. Jacques Derrida had a following in Communist Poland and was arrested for trading on the philosophical black market in former Czechoslovakia. Beijing today boasts an Institute of Post-Modern Studies, where you can talk of difference and desire without unduly alarming the authorities. Žižek himself is one of a high-powered circle of Ljubljana Lacanians, a man with active political interests in the new Slovenia.

This background is also perhaps relevant to his passion for the Real. Lacan, as we have seen, is not for Žižek a post-structuralist in the popular, packaged sense of the word ('spaghetti structuralism,' as Žižek scornfully dubs it), which means dissolving everything into discourse. On the contrary, the whole point of the Real is to give language the slip, block it from the inside, bend the signifier out of true. For Lacan, language is forced up against the wall of the Real and made to turn out its empty pockets. Žižek, who enjoys finding arcane meanings in bits of cliché, would doubtless bark 'Get Real!' to those for whom language is all there is. But this concern for what defeats totality, for the way desire gets thwarted, for how an autocratic authority sadistically enjoins us to enjoy that condition: all of this can surly be read against the background of that mass blockage of desire, along with a cynical invitation to the masses to hug their chains, which was bureaucratic Communism.

There is a parallel here with that other Eastern European heretic, Milan Kundera. In *The Unbearable Lightness of Being*, Kundera speaks of a contrast between the 'angelic' and the 'demonic,' the former signifying too much meaning and the latter too little. Totalitarian states are angelic, fearful of obscurity, dragging everything into luminous significance and instant legibility; the demonic, by contrast is marked by a cynical cackle which revolts against the tidy sense-making of tyranny by revelling in the brute meaninglessness of things. It is not hard to spot Lacan's Symbolic Order in the former and the Real in the latter, or to understand why the sheer contingency of the Real, its trick of disrupting closed symbolic systems with a remainder of unsatisfied desire, should have an appeal to an Eastern European intellectual. What one might call Lacan's ethical imperative — his injunction to the patient not to give up on his desire even while acknowledging its impossibility — sound rather like the position of Polish Solidarity in its darkest days.

Indeed, for Lacan, the psychoanalytic cure is a little like the achievement of political independence. What troubles us most deeply in Lacan's view is the fact that, though our desire is of the Other (i.e. drawn from the Other, as well as directed to it), we can never be entirely sure what it is that the Other is demanding of us, since any demand has to be interpreted, and so to be garbled by the duplicitous signifier. 'What do they want of me, what am I expected to be?' is the insistent query which for Lacan hollows our being into desire. The cured patient is the one who has given up on this unanswerable question, acknowledged that her desire is entirely self-grounding, embraced the utter contingency of her own being and relinquished the futile quest of having it confirmed from the outside. If this has a faint resemblance to getting out from under a political oppressor, it also, as Žižek reminds us, has more than a smack of the saint. The image of the cured patient, one might claim, is Samuel Richardson's *Clarissa*, who by the end of his novel has turned her face to the wall, renounced the claims of others and embraced her death by withdrawing her body from libidinal circulation. To be cured of your psychic ailments, you really need to be a saint, which is perhaps one reason why psychoanalysis is such a lengthy, precarious affair.

There is another sense in which Žižek's Marxist background is relevant. No acolyte of Lacan from Paris or Pittsburgh would have anything like Žižek's political *nous*, a faculty you develop spontaneously in a place where the political is the colour of everyday life. Lacan himself, who advances an essentially tragic philosophy of life, had a lofty contempt for politics, indeed for history as such; whereas Žižek, who fails for the most part to comment on his mentor's dandyish megalomania, is a post-Marxist who applies his psychoanalytic insights to racism, nationalism, anti-semitism, totalitarianism, the commodity form. It is hardly surprising that a psychoanalytic theorist of such virtuosity should have emerged from the ethnic conflicts of former Yugoslavia, just as Europe's previous most fruitful encounter between Marx and Freud was the product of the Frankfurt School on the run from Nazi anti-semitism.

Racism, nationalism, anti-semitism are where the abstruse categories of psychoanalysis are brought home to everyday political life. And Žižek, who was writing at one point with the Bosnian war on his doorstep, has a sense of the Realpolitik of the psyche quite foreign to the gentrified, consumerist, post-ideological Western world for which he has such proper contempt. If he is more unabashedly theoretical than the typical Anglo-Saxon intellectual is, he is also a lot more practical. He is even getting a little restive these days with his own post-Marxism, chiding its neglect of the economic in traditional Marxist style. He is startlingly casual — indeed, for such a profoundly sophisticated thinker, almost naïve — in the way that he moves so directly from the psychoanalytic to the political, a frontier along which many a fellow-theorist has preferred to pussyfoot. Fetishism, scapegoating, splitting, foreclosure, disavowal, idealizing, projection: if these are the familiar mechanisms of the Freudian psyche, they are also mass movements, political strategies, military campaigns. Writing during the Bosnian war in *Metastases of Enjoyment*[3] of a New Zealand tribe who invented a grotesque war-dance for the delectation of the visiting anthropologists, he notes that 'David Owen and companions are today's version of the expedition to the New Zealand tribe: they act and react exactly in the same way, overlooking how the entire spectacle of "old hatreds suddenly erupting in their primordial cruelty" is a dance for which the West is thoroughly responsible.

'I am convinced of my proper grasp of some Lacanian concept,' Žižek writes, 'only when I can translate it successfully into the current imbecility of popular culture'. His works are awash with allusions to detective fiction and David Lynch, movies and musicals. A particularly tricky aspect of Schelling's notion of freedom is illuminated by the Flintstones, while Kant's doctrine of the transcendental unity of apperception is exemplified by vampire novels. An aesthetic distinction between classical and avant-garde music is illustrated by whether or not the audience cough and shuffle at the end of a movement. Commentaries on the films of Hitchcock—Žižek's King Charles's Head, one might say—almost outnumber his analyses of Hegel. In a fine essay on *Psycho* in *Everything You Always Wanted to Know about Lacan (But Were Too Afraid to Ask Hitchcock)*,[4] a collection of Hitchcock essays by various hands, he treats us to a Lacanian analysis of the moment when the camera first looks down from above on the private eye being attacked by the disguised Anthony Perkins, then cuts to a shot of the stabbed detective hurtling backwards down the staircase. The bird's-eye shot, Žižek informs us, lays bare an apparently transparent reality, into which the 'Thing' or enigmatic murderer suddenly intrudes; what follows, shockingly, is a shot of the murder victim from the 'impossible' view of the Thing itself.

The striking thing of Žižek's use of popular culture is its lack of coyness. Unlike his wilfully hermetic Parisian *maître*, his writing is splendidly crisp and lucid, even if his books can be fearsomely difficult. The difficulties belong to the ideas, not the expression, a distinction between signified and signifier at which the wilder kind of post-structuralist would doubtless baulk. There is no sense that he is strenuously popularizing—or of some contrived Post-Modern pastiche; soap operas and Disney cartoons are just part of his intellectual furniture, objects of his promiscuous inquiries as familiar as God, Kant or consumerism. His style is deep and light simultaneously, shot through with an intense political seriousness but never at all portentous. His prose resonates with the feel of a markedly idiosyncratic personality, but is curiously without self-display. The fact that he is so compulsively obsessional about both Hitchcock and Lacan is a kind of tacit running joke, something so embarrassingly obtrusive that it would be boring for either author or reader even to mention it.

Indeed, jokes form some of Žižek's primary philosophical examples. He has a good line in sardonic East European political humour, as when he remarks that the difference between the Soviet Union and Yugoslavia was that, whereas in the former the people walked while their elected representatives drove cars, in the latter, more liberalized version of communism, the people themselves drove cars through their elected representatives. To illustrate the dialectic of presence and absence, he recounts the story of a guide conducting some visitors round an East European art gallery and halting before a painting entitled *Lenin in Warsaw*. There is no sign of Lenin in the picture; instead, it depicts Lenin's wife in bed with a handsome young member of the Central Committee. 'But where is Lenin?' inquire the bemused visitors, to which the guide gravely replies, 'Lenin is in Warsaw'.

Žižek thinks Hegel and Lacan entirely compatible, partly because he reads the former through the latter in a heretical deconstruction of Hegel's supposed holism. Indeed, the flavour of his mind is thoroughly Hegelian, continually on the prowl for antitheses inverting themselves into identities, in a set of dialectical guerrilla raids on common sense. Some random examples: it is not that order and disorder are opposites, but that the imposition of a (purely contingent) order on chaos is itself the highest mode of disorder. The Lacanian Other — the Symbolic Order, or language as a whole — can have no Other to itself, which is to say that there can be no ultimate guarantee of the field of meaning. Multiculturalism is just a kind of racism in reverse, respecting another's culture from the distancing, unchallenged vantage-point of one's own. The law must be irrational, since if there were reasons for obeying it, it would lose its absolute authority. The unconscious is not the opposite of consciousness, but the founding act of repression by which consciousness is established in the first place.

The following captures something of his characteristic intellectual style:

At first glance it would seem that the sausage in the hot dog wedges apart the two pieces of roll. But the roll itself is nothing but a "space" which the sausage creates around it, the phantasmal "frame" or support of the sausage without which it would vanish to nothing. On the other hand, the sausage itself can be seen as no more than an embodied gap between the two pieces of bread, the mere pretext or occasion which prevents them from ever uniting

This is my parody rather than Žižek's own words, but much odder passages are to be found in his work.

Žižek is especially deft-fingered when it comes to dismantling the opposition between the universal and the particular. The universal, he points out, must exclude particularity, and so can't really be as universal as it supposes. We have access to universals only because we are situated within a specific culture, a point which both rationalists and relativists might do will to ponder. Cultural relativism, Žižek notes, is much vexed by out supposed inability to gain access to the 'other'; but what if this other were inherently incomplete, and so in any case unknowable as a whole? What if what I share most deeply with the other is just the fact that I, too, am never wholly bound to my own cultural context but always to some degree out of joint with it? What I and the other have in common is the fact that there is always something which eludes our grasp (Lacan's 'big Other'), and it is in the overlapping of these twin absences that we can meet. It is when we are able to discern the blindspot of another culture, its point of failure, that we are most at one with it, since it is just such an internal limit which constitutes our own forms of life, too.

In his latest two books, Žižek has turned to the study of the German philosopher F.W.J. Schelling, who over the past few years has been shot from Teutonic obscurity to something like philosophical stardom. Žižek, naturally, finds a lot of Lacan in Schelling as he finds him in everything; but he also makes some rather extravagant claims for Schelling as a precursor of the 'entire post-Hegelian constellation,' from Marxism and existentialism to deconstruction and New Age obscurantism. He is especially fascinated by Schelling's highly esoteric theology — unsurprisingly in a way, for what is the Real, this kink or deviation at the heart of things without which they would not work, but the fortunate Fall or *felix culpa*? The Real is a psychoanalytic version of Original Sin, and Schelling boldly applies this notion to God as well, who like us is never fully himself, plagued by a foreign body at the core of his being which is (one should have guessed it) precisely what allows him to be the Almighty. That the Creator is also afflicted by the Real is perhaps some small comfort to his creatures. It is curious that conservative pessimists who find no problem with the doctrine of Original Sin would doubtless dismiss both Lacan and Žižek as theoretical nihilists.

'If we were able to penetrate the exterior of things,' Schelling comments, 'we would see that the true stuff of all life and existence is the horrible'. One can see, then, why he is Žižek's sort of thinker. But Žižek never really takes time off from his explorations to reflect on just what a hideous view of human life he is delivering us, or on how this is compatible with the political dissent which he clearly still embraces. How is 'Lacanian radical' not to be as oxymoronic a phrase as 'military intelligence'? The view from the Real is admittedly no more horrible than what Anglican vicars are supposed to believe, but then Anglican vicars are not noted for their political radicalism. Just as human existence for Lacan is the fantasy by which we plug the terrifying void of the Real, so Žižek's chirpy wit and anecdotal relish serve in part to mask the obscene vision of humanity he offers.

If the only topic psychoanalysis recognizes is enjoyment, the same might finally be said of Žižek the writer. His books have an enviable knock of making Kant or Kierkegaard sound riotously exciting; his writing bristles with difficulties but never serves up a turgid sentence. The demotic companionability of his style is an implicit rebuke to the high-minded terrorism of so much French theory. Lacan may insist that the analyst is an empty signifier, that he holds no secret key to the patient's unhappiness, but his posturing rhetoric belies any such disavowal. 'Enjoy!' is Žižek's implicit injunction to the reader, as he shifts within a single chapter from Mozart to time travel, hysteria to Judaism, Marx to Marlboro ads, while managing somehow to sustain a coherent argument. In his case too, however, form and content are subtly at variance. The mercurial sparkle of his work is at odds with its bleak, mechanically recurrent content, for which enjoyment, in the Real, is where we encounter the least delectable truths of all.

One of his latest offerings, *The Ticklish Subject*, is not a book for the faint-hearted. Its ideal reader would need to be familiar with the minor works of Schelling, the politics of globalization and the movies of David Lynch. True to its author's inimitably idiosyncratic style, the book mixes expositions of Hegel, Kant, Marx and Lacan with jokes, anecdotes from Slovenian politics, comments on Bill Gates, virtual reality and the ozone layer, allusions to mass culture, and observation on the psychopathology of everyday late-capitalist life. Yet if the subject-matter is sometimes ferociously opaque, the style could hardly be more supple, lucid and, again, companionable.

As perceptive about Monica Lewinsky as about Vladimir Lenin, Žižek proceeds here in his customary, mildly maniacal manner to shake the foundations of his reader's commonsensical assumptions. Much taken with the psychoanalytic category of perversity, he is a prime intellectual instance of it himself. A typical Žižekian move would be to demonstrate with uncanny plausibility that sleep was result of having beds around the place, not *vice versa*. In fact it takes this kind of chiasmic mind, fascinated by ironies and dialectical inversions, to propose a bold rehabilitation of the Cartesian subject, as Žižek does in this study. In today's cultural climate, to speak up for this genderless, disembodied entity is as audacious as urging the dietary value of lard or denouncing car parking for the disabled. Caught in a pincer movement between Heidegger and Ryle, Wittgenstein and behaviourism, the Cartesian subject seems as *passé* as Roy Rogers; yet Žižek, forever allergic to postmodern fads, brushes perversely against the grain.

It is not, to be sure, quite Descartes' thinking thing which he is out to reinstate. What he challenges instead, as one who once penned a doctoral thesis on Heidegger, is the whole existential, phenomenological insistence on our worldly embodiedness, on the fact that our reflections always take place within some concrete project or life-world. This is true as far as it goes, but in Žižek's eyes it is also a form of defence against the embarrassments of the unconscious. The human subject may be situational, but it is also eccentric, out of joint, the joker in Nature's pack. There is that within us which spins on its own sweet way regardless of the life-world or the reality principle, and its name is the unconscious.

In a typical Žižekian inversion, then, the spectral Cartesian ego is reborn, but this time as its exact opposite, the id. What precedes our being-in-the-world for psychoanalytic thought is not some self-brooding cogito, but something far more fearful: that chaotic, 'preontological' domain of drives which Hegel calls the 'night of the world,' out of which egoic reality is them constituted. A 'psychotic' withdrawal from the world is for this line of thought at the very core of the world-creating subject. There is indeed a sort of Cartesian spirit, forever dislocated from the world, but it is a form of madness.

As we have seen, the Real in Žižek's view is the traumatic core of 'obscene enjoyment' at the heart of the subject — that monstrous excess or otherness, born of the deadly complicity of Law and desire, which makes us what we are but forever eludes our grasp; and what we know as reality is, in Lacan's view, simply the set of fantasies with which we fill in this constitutive hole at the heart of being. One name for this void, for that which can never be adequately symbolized and which is the ruin of all our attempts at totality, is the subject itself. Again there is the Lacanian ethical injunction not to give up on this desire, but to remain faithful to it despite its 'impossibility,' and this to emerge somewhere on the other side of its pathological grip.

In an extraordinary chapter entitled 'The Politics of Truth,' Žižek explores the theological implications of this doctrine in a brilliant excursus on law, death, sin and the flesh in the writings of St. Paul. Christ is one of those figures (Sophocles' Oedipus and Shakespeare's Lear are others) who, having encountered the death drive as the ultimate limit of human experience, have passed beyond that humanity into a realm of monstrous destitution which is the only conceivable basis of a new, transformed human order. Jesus is the *skandalon* or stumbling block rejected only to become the cornerstone, and his descent into hell is the Christian version of Hegel's psychotic 'night of the world'. In a boldly imaginative move, Žižek claims that something like this also lies behind the Lacanian interpretation of the psychoanalytic 'cure'.

Madness, desire, monstrosity: these are postmodern motifs *par excellence*. But Žižek is that most perverse of all 'postmodern' thinkers, one who remains stubbornly committed to an Enlightenment ideal of universal emancipation. Being reared in Communist Yugoslavia may prejudice you against totalities, which is no doubt one reason why the anti-totalizing Lacan has his attractions; but it also allows you a sniff of real politics, in which Žižek has been actively involved, and consequent impatience with phoney postmodern radicalisms. The book includes a scorching critique of the covert racism of so-called multiculturalism, along with a good deal else to nettle the purveyors of identity politics. With a candour rare in these devious, discursive days, it accuses such radicals of evading the whole question of global capitalism, intent as they are on securing their 'life-style' niches within it. If resurrecting the Cartesian subject is a resolutely unmodish move, calling for a resistance to global capitalism is even more bravely out of joint with the times. *The Ticklish Subject* is a magisterial work from one of the major philosophers of our age — though most English philosophers have probably never heard of him.

TERRY EAGLETON
University of Manchester

NOTES

1   Slavoj Žižek, *The Indivisible Remainder* (London, Verso, 1996); *The Abyss of Freedom/Ages of the World* (Ann Arbor, Michigan, University of Michigan Press, 1997); *The Plague of Fantasies* (London, Verso, 1997); *the Ticklish Subject* (London, Verso, 1999).
2   Slavoj Žižek, *The Sublime Object of Ideology* (London, Verso, 1989).
3   Slavoj Žižek, *The Metastases of Enjoyment* (London, Verso, 1994).
4   Slavoj Žižek, *Everything You Always Wanted to Know about Lacan (But Were Too Afraid to Ask Hitchcock)* (London, Verso, 1992).

Has Oedipus Signed Off (or Struck Out)?: Žižek, Lacan and the Field of Cyberspace

Costello: I'm only asking you. *Who*'s the guy on first base?
Abbott: That's right.
(Abbott and Costello, 'Who's on First?' [1936])[1]

Taking the Field

Perhaps in part because of the attention he gives to cutting-edge popular culture, Slavoj Žižek enjoys a celebrity status that is unique in the field of cultural theory, his reputation as both flamboyant showman and intellectual heavy-hitter confirmed by the colourful moniker — 'The Giant of Ljubljana' — which seems to confer the charisma of a popular sports-hero on this Lacanian philosopher.

But decades before Lacan's own grandstand play diagrammed Žižek's field as the relay of intersubjective desire around four bases (in the schema L), popular culture had already produced a peerless demonstration of sliding subjectivity, circulating in a diamond-shaped semantic field.[2] I am, of course, referring to Abbott and Costello's classic routine on baseball, 'Who's on First?' (1936), which hilariously muddles meaning and position: the straight man Abbott pitches a slippery signifier ('Who') to his hopelessly confused partner Costello, unable to catch its meaning, none the less gives merry chase to the shifter as it rounds the bases.

Costello: Look Abbott, if you're the coach, you must know all the players.
Abbott: I certainly do.
Costello: So you'll have to tell me their names, and then I'll know who's playing on the team.
Abbott: [...] Well, let's see, we have on the bags ... Who's on first, What's on second, I Don't Know's on third ...
Costello: That's what I want to find out.

Lacanian theory might say that Abbott is invested by his interlocutor as Obstacle/Other or symbolic authority, the Subject Supposed to Know ('if you're the coach, you must know all the players'). But from the opening exchange, Costello misrecognizes the straightman's straight answer, pitched right across the plate, as his own question bounced back to him. And one could hardly ask for a livelier demonstration of the play of the Lacanian object, where the shifter 'who' is both an other (the object of desire, the *objet petit a*) and an Other (locus of the symbolic register) — whose open 'O' is ground zero of the questioner's uncertainty.

Meanwhile, back in the diamond-shaped infield, the crowd always enjoys the vociferous 'in your face' wrangles between player and umpire — the altercations revealing that meaning is always up for grabs, that the player's demand is always excessive, and that even the Subject Supposed to Know . . . is 'blind' (according to the traditional insult hurled at the umpire from the stands).

Even in this brief excursion, it is clear that baseball lingo redounds with images suggestive of the Freudian field. In fact, in the sort of happy coincidence that Lacan loved to exploit in his own parables, the shape of both playing fields is a diamond: for the *losange* takes pride of place not only in the doubled triangle of Lacan's schema L, but also in Lacan's algorithmic notation of the subject's relation to an object perpetually in flight ($\$◇a$). Like Lacan's own spectacular performance in the seminar, aimed at exposing the limitations of the '*sujet supposé savoir*' to an onlooking arena (the verb *supposer* itself foregrounding an effect of positioning), Abbott and Costello's performance illustrates the axiom that the 'Other [as Ultimate Answer Man] does not exist'.

In his turn, when 'the Giant of Ljubljana' makes his entrance onto the field at the end of the twentieth century, his commentary on the Lacanian order as the scopic field of a reciprocal gaze — where the object looks *back* — emphasizes Lacan's teaching that subjectivity is always positional and interactive, determined by slide and shift, feint and theft. Again, baseball serves up an object lesson illustrating the point; for the art of stealing bases, honoured in an official statistic of the game, is above all a contest between opposing subjects, pitcher and runner, trying to 'fake each other out'. And Žižek has described Lacan's notion of the imaginary duel between subjects in strikingly similar terms, adding that the imaginary game of feint progresses to 'symbolic deception,' feigning to the next power as it were, when caught in the field of an intersubjective gaze, at once 'interactive' and 'interpassive,' objectified and objectifying: 'human feigning is the feigning of feigning itself: in imaginary deception, I simply present a false image of myself, while in symbolic deception, I present a true image and count on its being taken for a lie' (*The Plague of Fantasies*, 139).[3]

Appropriately enough, this example is itself situated in a chain of intertextual references. For Žižek replays Lacan's position on symbolic deception and opacity (spelled out in Seminars III and XI); while Lacan has nabbed *his* example from Freud (*Jokes and their Relation to the Unconscious*), who in turn got his example from 'tradition' (Freud relays the old Jewish joke about two old men on the road to Krakow, who seek to outwit each other by appearing to lie while telling the truth). This kind of circulation insists in Lacan's seminars, and it is a strategy that the Giant of Ljubljuna has learned well from the coach. And in *Looking Awry*, moreover, Žižek points out that while any theory is contingent on position, and is received in a series of intertextual relays, this is perhaps especially true of the position of the 'official' who is 'supposed to know' the answers, but who is always partially blind, thanks to the opacity that insists in the intersubjective gaze itself, the fact that 'you never look at me from the place where I see you'. Even the umpire can do no more than confer an always subjective meaning on a field of vision that is always skewed and partial.

I want to turn now to Žižek's essay on digital interactivity/inter-passivity ('Is it Possible to Traverse the Fantasy in Cyberspace?'), in order to read the essay as a play-by-play reflection on the consequences of positioning itself, in the 'whole new ball game' of a new century where subjects play by relaying bits and bytes.[4]

Or is it so new? Žižek's play of positions may in fact reveal that the rules of the game have not changed quite as much as it may appear: for who's on first may still be an effect of 'who' or 'what' is on second and third, and how and why they got there — as well as the pitch of the sportscaster who is calling the plays as he sees them.

Changing the Line-up

Costello: All I'm trying to find out is ... *What*'s the guy's name on first base.
Abbott: Well, don't change the players around.

In his first essay on the digital field, ('The Unbearable Closure of Being' in *The Plague Of Fantasies*), Žižek takes on what he sees as two post-modern 'myths' about cyberspace: 1) the perception that cyberspace provides a kind of delirious aesthetic media experience, possibly affording a more intense sensual experience than that of 'RL' (real life) itself 2) the perception that cyberspace interaction in the post-modern mode of simulation provokes a confusion of the domains of 'RL' (real life) and 'VR' (virtual reality).

To these two positions, Žižek adds a third as elaboration and refinement, attributed respectively to Sherry Turkle and Allucquère Rosanne Stone: the assumption that the experience of cyberspace may provide a liberating potential for the post-modern 'decentered' subject. Žižek mounts a convincing critique of all three assumptions, based on the Lacanian perception that the subject in cyberspace is after all an 'avatar' of the ego, which is itself an illusory entity, merely covering a split that grounds all subjectivity in a division far more radical than that characterized by 'post-modern' theory as a decentering in simulated space.

Having voiced his objections to these three takes on virtual subjectivity, Žižek proposes a fourth position, as a sort of correction of post-modern notions of the subject. For he concedes that, even if cyberspace doesn't 'decenter' an always-already split subject in any radical way, the ascendance of the virtual may indeed harbour some liberating social potential, as a kind of transitional field that may attenuate some of the hard knocks of real life. (Žižek even suggests, apparently without irony, that we may someday see the settling of war in a virtual arena.)

It is noteworthy that the structure of the first essay is reproduced in Žižek's second piece on the digital culture, 'Is it Possible to Traverse the Fantasy in Cyberspace?' (Hereafter 'Traversing the Fantasy'/ TF), which also traces a triadic structure where three bases subsequently open up to a fourth base, or conclusion. For in both cases Žižek's own constructed playing field is a tetrahedron or diamond uncannily reminiscent of Lacan's *losange*, but positioning Žižek himself as the player who will reach home base, scoring the winning point or at least crediting himself for 'bringing the others in'.

Significantly, Žižek's opening move is a self-positioning in the theoretical field:

As a psychoanalytically oriented (Lacanian) philosopher, let me begin with the question one expects an analyst to raise: what are the consequences of cyberspace for Oedipus — that is, for the mode of subjectivization that psychoanalysis conceptualized as the Oedipus complex and its dissolution? (TF *The Žižek Reader*, 111)

Here Žižek announces that his position and his topic is predetermined by the expectations of his readers ('let me begin with the question one *expects* an analyst to raise'). This is entirely appropriate for a Lacanian, of course, because Lacan himself insists that our own subjective position is always taken up in the pre-existing field of the Other's desire, and that our own stance is in part determined by our anticipation of the Other's move. In other words, it is to be expected, when 'the Giant of Ljubljana' steps up to the plate to comment on millennial culture, that he acknowledge himself as a player.

The problem, however, is that Žižek also sets himself up as umpire, professing something like neutrality and even-handedness in this opening formulation. But a closer look reveals that even in this opening play the game may already be up for Oedipus: by putting the verb 'conceptualize' in the past tense, Žižek has already subtly 'pitched' the discussion from a post-oedipal angle, at the same time that he pitches Oedipus as a 'complex,' rather than as a theory of subject-formation. Like any theorist playing on the diamond-shaped field of intersubjectivity, then, Žižek has an angle or 'bias'. Yet Žižek's position on Oedipus would seem to reposition twenty-first century psychoanalytic theory itself somewhere *outside* the Freudian field, a move which, given Lacan's own insistence on 'returning to Freud,' is radical indeed. How and why does Žižek get from here to there?

First of all, he changes the line-up from essay one to essay two, adding new players; indeed, in the second go-round, the emphasis has been shifted to Oedipus, the new star-player who none the less seems to be on the verge of being thrown out of the game. But an even more startling change is Žižek's own pre-emptive 'strike' in the second piece, where he pathologizes all three 'predominant' views on Oedipus, in one sweeping ruling.

Clinically it is easy to categorize these three versions as psychosis, perversion, and hysteria: the first version claims that cyberspace entails universalized psychosis; according to the second one, cyberspace opens up the liberating perspective of globalized multiple perversion; the third one claims that cyberspace remains within the confines of the enigmatic Other that hystericizes the subject. (TF, 116)

This surprising move raises the question of just what the stakes of this play may be, even 'beyond Oedipus'. For Oedipus is in a sense only brought into the game as a player who has already been thrown out of it: 'The predominant doxa today is that cyberspace explodes, or at least potentially undermines the reign of Oedipus, announcing instead some new post-oedipal libidinal economy' (TF, 110).

In any case, Žižek underscores Oedipus' status as 'has-been' by attributing this new '*post*-oedipal' economy to the players on *both* first and second base in his essay. But on third, Žižek introduces a new argument into the line-up, which he calls 'the assertion of the continuity of cyberspace with the oedipal mode of subjectivation' (113). This third base seems to be given some importance in its positioning adjacent to 'home' (third is the base from which the runner is always poised to score), as well as in its explicit focus on Oedipus, the topic of the essay. But whereas the coach 'names names' in filling bases one (Virilio, Vattimo, Baudrillard) and two (Stone and Turkle) in his new line-up, he leaves 'third' curiously empty, characterizing it elliptically as the position of 'some rare, if none the less penetrating theoreticians,' whose identity is referenced only in an endnote.

Now I can go no further in this discussion without acknowledging the stakes of my own position here. For Žižek's analyses of culture have consistently figured prominently in my effort at resiting Oedipus in millennial culture, a focus of my work for some years.[5] But I am 'interested' in this new essay in a much more direct way as well, since the essay that Žižek's footnote sites/cites as the sole example of the nameless theorist(s) 'on third' is in fact an early version of 'Is Oedipus On-line?,' the title chapter of my forthcoming book. One motivation for my discussion here, then, is the desire to respond to Žižek's reading, since I think he gets my argument wrong by misplacing and replacing its terms.

But in any case, I want to point out that by appending his own view to the three he evaluates, constructing a field with *four* bases, Žižek performs a move which, consciously or not, recalls Lacan's own iterations of a dimensionalized triangle, doubled/expanded to four base positions. In fact, Lacan quite literally opens up the oedipal triangle in the schema L (named after the Greek lambda, and resembling a 'Z'), by unhinging and unfolding one of its three sides. In other words, the fourth base is created by splitting the locus of the subject into (at least) two positions at once — the barred subject and 'imaginary' ego. This unfolding of the oedipal triangle continues in his work in seminar XV (as yet untranslated) on the transference as a process occurring around four bases. (In fact, Lacan refers there to the structure of the analytic transference as a 'tetrahedron,' remarking on a *rotation* of subject positions among the symbolic, imaginary, and real registers; and these registers are themselves depicted in a series of embedded triangular configurations in a number of diagrams of progressive complexity. The details, while intriguing, need not be rehearsed here — and indeed cannot be reproduced here, since the 'authorized' translation has not yet appeared.)

Lacan's main point is that the process of transference ultimately repositions the subject in the position of the analyst, as s/he moves into a position to 'see' that the Subject *Supposed* to Know in fact does not possess superior knowledge. The subject thus begins to 'analyze' for herself, as the new subject of a more complete, if always incomplete, knowledge. Similarly, in Freud's account of the passing of the Oedipus complex ('The Dissolution of the Oedipus Complex' [1924]), the subject accedes to the law and rotates to the position of authority, by re-enacting the process with a new generation, where s/he is positioned in turn as the parental 'know-it-all'.

If I insist on the three-to-four, triangle-to-*losange* structure that subtends Lacan's subject-formation, as well as his account of the analytic situation, it is to suggest that Žižek's essay may finally have implications about positionality itself — and about 'thirdness' as an attribute of fourthness. Thus if I reargue the question of Oedipus Internaut here, it is not simply to declare Oedipus on-line or Žižek off-base. For Žižek's new essay in fact provides a refreshing contrast to the doomsday tenor of much millennial theory ('the social order is dead! the machines have already won!'). To his credit, Žižek emphasizes the social and material conditions of cyberspace as crucial factors in considering the effects of digital interaction on intersubjective relations. Indeed, rather than acceding to the demand to pronounce a ready-made judgement about whether cyberspace is 'good' or 'bad' for the human subject, 'the Giant' of theory quite rightly questions the premises of the question itself. But I do want to challenge the umpire on his removal of Oedipus from this game, as an exclusion which may risk removing Freud himself from the thick of the action on Freud Field. For while I think we can cheer Žižek on for pursuing a social agenda in his work, I suggest that he cannot make his point by short-circuiting his argument, forgetting to touch base with its Freudian sources.

Making the Double Play

Costello: What's the guy's name on first base?
Abbott: No. What is on second.
Costello: I'm not asking you who's on second.
Abbott: Who's on *first*.

Žižek begins his critique of cyber-Oedipus with a double play of sorts, combining the two scenarios that he says describe 'the end of Oedipus,' even while differentiating these two positions according to the base of the theorist ('Of course, the mode of perception of this "end" of O depends on the standpoint of the theoretician'[111]).

About the theorists that he visits 'at first,' whom he names only parenthetically (Baudrillard, Virilio, and Vattimo), Žižek writes:

> First, there are those who see in this a dystopian prospect of individuals regressing to pre-symbolic psychotic immersion, of losing the symbolic distance that sustains the minimum of critical/ reflective attitude (the idea that the computer functions as a maternal Thing that swallows the subject, who entertains an attitude of incestuous fusion towards it). (111)

In other words, the ascendance of virtual simulacra is considered a dangerous lure by this 'dystopian' contingent. Now, the opening section of my own essay makes a similar point, highlighting the 'cyber-chosis' of the 'panic philosophers' (Baudrillard, Virilio, and others), and maintaining that their end-of-the-world scenarios have much in common with Freud's description of paranoia in the famous Schreber case. Žižek seems to rehearse that argument here, seconding my characterization of Baudrillard's thematic of lost dimensionality as a crisis in the symbolic dimension.[6] And Žižek's evocation of 'the Maternal Thing that swallows the subject' also echoes a passage in 'Oedipus On-line,' where I refer to Ray Barglow's image of the cybernaut 'mesmerized and stymied' by 'the addictive lure of the Mother Board to which one is connected for hours on end' (OO, 90). But there are a number of significant differences between our two assessments, differences which, in my view, contribute to Žižek's tendency to veer off base in his evaluation of the fantasy in cyberspace.

1) Although Žižek limits himself to three players 'on first' as representatives of the 'psychotic' interpretation of cyber-subjectivity, this dystopian view is in fact extremely widespread in millennial theory. Indeed, the selection of three very well-known theorists (Baudrillard, Virilio, Vattimo) as figures whose names may stand parenthetically for the whole body of their work — in a kind of metonymic shorthand that assumes the reader's familiarity with their theory — causes this position to appear unduly authoritative, and even perhaps masculinized as well, especially since Žižek's treatment all but elides the large number of feminist theorists who share this 'dystopian' reading. (Recent books by Anne Balsamo and Claudia Springer, for

instance, criticize cyber culture as a domain which is masculinist, and even misogynist, objectifying women — as in the sci-fi trope of the 'cyber-babe'-and commodifying sexuality — as in the booming on-line 'bride business'.)

But Žižek's threesome on first omits many other high-profile dystopian theorists of modern culture as well, since one could well include Foucault, Guy De Bord, and Deleuze (Mr. Anti-Oedipus himself) as dystopian philosophers and critics of disciplinary high-tech society, even when cyberspace is not their specific focus. (One could also add more popular theorists of cyberspace to this list of dystopians: Mark Dery, Adam Parfrey, Arthur and Marilouise Kroker, all decry something like 'the death of the social'.) However, the fact that *none* of these theorists argue that we are witnessing the 'end of Oedipus' at the millennial cusp — whatever their appraisal of the ethical valence of psychoanalysis itself — suggests that Žižek's alignment of dystopian millennial theory with the theory of the end of Oedipus may not be viable.

2) The second problem with Žižek's position 'on first' concerns the location of the psychotic tendency itself. For rather than insisting that the *subject* in cyberspace is somehow necessarily psychotic — which may plug in to defeatist appraisals of human 'helplessness' in the new age — I think that one might consider this paranoid theory as an overestimation of the Imaginary that follows from the standpoint of the *theorist*. For the panic philosophers like Virilio and Baudrillard may claim to lament a loss of human mooring in 'real life,' but they really seem to indulge themselves in an elegy for the (mythical, illusory) transcendental human subject, the identity of the 'self' in the good old days when boundaries were clear and rules of conduct were defined, including the rules of our 'naturally' gendered positions.

But in fact Žižek's own discussion shows signs of this nostalgic temptation. For he asserts that the 'psychotic' or dystopian reading is 'at its strongest when it insists on the difference between appearance and simulacrum' (111). And he goes on to assert that what is really lost in Virilio and Vattimo's 'post-modern Brave New World of universalized simulacra,' is *appearance* in the Kantian sense: 'appearance is thus the domain not simply of phenomena, but of those "magic moments" in which another, noumenal dimension momentarily 'appears' in ('shines through') some empirical, contingent phenomena' (111).

In this framing, it is no longer clear whether Žižek is simply *explaining* the position of the dystopians 'at their strongest'; *criticizing* that position (to which he refers in passing as a 'sentimental platitude');

or perhaps actually *advocating* that position. In other words, the lack of attribution of the point of view tends to permit Žižek to 'slide' from the position of observer to that of advocate, as he seems to do in this assertion: 'Therein lies the problem with cyberspace and virtual reality: what virtual reality threatens is not reality, which is dissolved in the multiplicity of its simulacra, but on the contrary, appearance itself' (111).

Žižek's actual affiliation with the first base that he seems to refute becomes more apparent when he affirms that what is missing in virtual reality is not material reality itself, but a certain 'symbolic efficacy' that depends on retaining a kind of mystery of designation:

The crucial difference between the simulacrum (overlapping with the Real) and appearance is easily discernible in the domain of sexuality, in the guise of the distinction between pornography and seduction: pornography 'shows it all,' 'real sex,' and for that very reason produces mere simulacra of sexuality, while the process of seduction consists entirely in the play of appearances, hints and promises, and thereby evokes the elusive domain of the supra-sensible sublime Thing. (112)

In fact, Žižek's writings elsewhere (particularly in *Looking Awry*) insist that the problem with pornography is that too much is shown and known, as opposed to the process outlined here, 'the process of seduction [which] consists entirely in the play of appearances, hints and promises,' which allows us to persist in our fantasies of 'the elusive domain of the supra-sensible sublime thing'.

And this fear of over-exposure as a deadening of some ineffable mystery echoes another fear expressed in both *Looking Awry* and *The Plague of Fantasies* — that a repressive hyper-symbolic order will result in a totalitarian surveillance: 'The Other must not know all. This is an appropriate definition of the nontotalitarian social field' (*Looking Awry*, 73). While this is a compelling formulation, Žižek's own position shows that it 'veils' a certain sentimentality about the mysteries of the sublime, buttressed by the concept of a true 'appearance' that shows itself in fleeting and privileged moments of revelation.

A final problem with Žižek's first base position is his simultaneous qualification of this standpoint as post-oedipal (as a 'libidinal economy beyond Oedipus') and pre-oedipal (entailing 'the threat of fusion with the Maternal Thing'). Even if this logical contradiction could be resolved, neither of these two states — 'pre-oedipal' implosion or post-oedipal 'psychosis' — may be considered '*beyond* Oedipus,' since the first regresses to 'before Oedipus,' and the second — 'psychosis' — is a symptom of a defensive reaction to the threat posed by the oedipal order itself.

In a sense, in stealing onto first base alongside his players, Žižek seems to keep Oedipus in the game.

What's on Second?

Žižek's second example of the 'end of Oedipus' is problematic for some of the same reasons. For both Stone and Turkle make arguments that are much more detailed and subtle than Žižek's brief reference acknowledges: these are no naïve utopians, enchanted with every aspect of cyber-culture. (For instance, Turkle discusses the problem of on-line crime and its psychological impact; while Stone's work performs a provocative analysis of cultural phenomena such as the attraction of the gothic in cyber-culture, as an effect of millennial anxiety about miscegenation, blurred gender boundaries and diseases of the blood.)[7] The short shrift that Žižek gives to these arguments is also somewhat suspect from a gender perspective, for the two theorists 'on second' are named with the familiar forms of their (feminine) given names ('Sandy Stone' and 'Sherry Turkle') while the male theorists on first are referenced more formally. In other words, if the first base is unduly masculinized in Žižek's presentation, as I've suggested, the 'post-modern' position 'on second' is both feminized and trivialized in a move that just may be related to Žižek's generally dismissive and negative view of 'post-modern' theories of the subject.

But the major problem with Žižek's alignment of Stone and Turkle is more fundamental. For in point of fact, neither Stone nor Turkle actually focuses on the end of Oedipus, as Žižek suggests. (Donna Haraway does focus on a 'post-oedipal, post-gender' societal organization, but Žižek fails to mention her work.) In fact, Stone does not really treat that status of psychoanalysis at all — her work is an historical and cultural chronicle of the origins of the internet at the juncture between two California cultures (Silicon Valley and New Age counter-culture); and Freud is not even cited in her index.

The misreading of Turkle is even more puzzling, for her work is actually extremely positive about psychoanalysis, including its future viability in analyzing subject-formation, and its continuity with many of the concerns of the information age. In fact, Turkle musters psychoanalysis as an ally in the resistance to a certain narrow positivism, suggesting that some aspects of modern cybernetic research be combined with psychoanalysis to help in understanding the decentered subject of millennial culture (*Life on the Screen*, [140]: 'connectionism can also help psychoanalysis undermine centrality and unitary views of the ego'. Far from mounting a critique of psychoanalysis, Turkle actually critiques a certain repressive effect of the patriarchal transcendental ego which Freudian theory helps to undermine).

Again, baseball lingo provides an apt term for the kind of move that Žižek performs here: it is a double play (two players are caught 'off-base' and ruled 'out' in a single relay of throws along the baseline). At the same time, there is a chiasmus in Žižek's own move. For he subtly (and no doubt unintentionally) elevates the first (masculinized) position, associating it with a 'strong version' of the Kantian notion of appearance — even while he seems to want to *refute* this position. Conversely, he seems to dismiss and misrepresent the second 'feminized' position — even while he appears to be *advocating* a version of it, as 'perversion,' in his conclusion. So this double play subtly steals first base by appropriating the position of the dystopians; and it steals into second as well, by 'correcting' its 'perverse' argument in the name of a certain authority or rigor.

Finally, Žižek's double play concerning 'the end of Oedipus' seems completely to overlook a crucial point: the original Oedipus to which Freud refers (Sophocles' *Oedipus Rex*) could itself have been subtitled 'The End of Oedipus,' since it shows the mythical tragic hero as exiled, done in by fate. Freud's infamous 'family romance,' laid on to the Sophoclean tragedy, describes a shift: from *Oedipus Rex* to *Oedipus Complex*. Thus Freud's own theory is already a postscript, a repositioning of Oedipus beyond (the mythical, literary) Oedipus, opening with the question of how each new human subject in fact *avoids* the tragic Oedipal model of incest and parricide.

And Freud's own theory on 'oedipal subject-formation,' in any case, already implies the two positions that Žižek sketches (as the dystopian and utopian versions, respectively, of 'the end of Oedipus'). For Freud's own version of the post-oedipal subject, in the 'The Dissolution of the Oedipus Complex' (1924) as well as in his work on psychosis, shows the consequences of a failure to resolve the castration complex, resulting in a foreclosure (of the primal scene, or of 'castration' or wounding): indeed, we could say that a dystopian oedipal consequence ('*Oedipus Wrecks*, The Tragedy'?) is enacted by Schreber, the Wolf Man, and other tragic heroes of psychosis. The second more felicitous scenario of a successful move 'beyond Oedipus' ('Oedipus *Wrecks*, the Comedy?') is likewise elaborated in many key Freudian texts, such as *Totem and Taboo, Jokes and their Relation to the Unconscious* and 'Creative Writers and Daydreaming,' which detail compelling, moving, and significant human endeavours (in such phenomena as joking, creative writing, play, literature, even the exogamous pollination or inmixing of different cultures).

As I have argued elsewhere, the best example of Freud's cultural theory is perhaps still his account of the transgressive activity of joking: for as Freud insists, joking breaks laws and re-establishes them simultaneously, but avoids tragic conflict by re-routing deadly hostile impulses along a route of substitutive conciliation. In Freud's account of joking, as in the classic oedipal scenario, a dyadic structure of seduction or conquest is opened to a triadic circuit of circumvention, thanks to the intervention of the outsider who acts as both obstacle and facilitator, ushering the subject into a social order beyond the closed (incestuous) fusion.

In other words, since Freud's Oedipus is already 'beyond Oedipus,' do we need the Žižekian move 'traversing the fantasy'?

On Coming in Third

Abbott: *Who*'s on first?
Costello: I don't know.
Abbott: *He*'s on third, we're not talking about him.

Žižek introduces my essay, 'Is Oedipus On-line?,' in an oblique reference:

However, opposed to both versions of 'cyberspace as the end of Oedipus' are some rare, if none the less penetrating, theoreticians who assert the continuity of cyberspace with the oedipal mode of subjectivization. (113)

This statement is annotated in a footnote, albeit laconically, and with the title abbreviated ('See Jerry Aline Flieger, "Oedipus On-line?" [*Pretextes* 1/6, 1997]). But while the text refers to 'some rare if penetrating theoreticians,' in the plural, the reference cites only this one example. (Incidentally, I would nominate Lyotard, Turkle, Haraway and the Žižek of *Looking Awry* himself, to share third base.) In any case, this lack of direct engagement is curious, since Žižek in fact performs a close reading of my essay, without directly acknowledging the dialogue.

My opening paragraph opens this lopsided exchange, citing Žižek up front:

> In a recent lecture at Columbia University, Slavoj Žižek coined a millennial aphorism that foregrounds the equivocal status of being in the information age: 'We are what we want, in cyberspace'. (OO, 81)

Žižek responds to this opening pitch by citing my citation of him in the anonymous single quotation style that obscures embedded reference: 'Yes, in cyberspace, 'you can be whatever you want'; you are free to choose a symbolic identity (a screen persona), but you must choose one in a way which will always betray you, which will never be fully adequate' (115). And there is an even more explicit echo in this relay:

> (Flieger, 'Is Oedipus On-line?'): This provocation, which recasts ontological status as an effect of virtual desire, explains why some bimillennials are still reading Freud, *to discover if our 'postsociety' has in fact succeeded in replacing interface for face-to-face.* (80)
>
> (Žižek, 'Traversing the Fantasy'): In short, *interface means that my relationship to the Other is never face-to-face.* (114)

Žižek goes on to detail another major focus of my argument — the convergence of the Schema L with the 'configuration' of intersubjective cyberspace:

> (Flieger, OO, 91): We may think of the zigzagging pass of desire in the Schema L as a kind of electronic path, where our own messages return to us in inverted form. (Žižek, TF, 115) It thus seems that cyberspace materializes directly the so-called Schema L elaborated by Lacan in the early fifties.

The intimate conversational volley with 'Is Oedipus On-line?' continues for several pages in Žižek's piece, culminating in a passage where my essay's title itself (as misquoted in the footnote) is deployed as a metonymy for the third base position: 'There is, however, a sense in which 'Oedipus On-line' no long functions as Oedipus proper' (114).

Indeed. My central point, in fact, is that 'Oedipus proper' is not the fundamental (or 'proper') structure in Freud himself, but is already an elaboration of a more radical subjectifying process, encountered throughout Freud's most challenging essays on culture, with implications that go far beyond the gender and culture-bound casting of Oedipus as castration complex.

Thus my work arguably 'comes in last' in Žižek's essay in more ways than the matter of attribution. Yet it is somehow peculiarly appropriate that Žižek has placed 'Oedipus On-line' third in his own line-up, since my argument there, as Žižek himself points out obliquely, is about 'thirdness' itself as a site introducing both complexity and context into any intersubjective relation, as well as exteriority or exile — whereby the Other is 'out in left field'. Žižek sums up my argument about 'thirdness' as a kind of screen:

> Cyberspace retains the fundamental oedipal structure of an intervening Third Order, which, in its very capacity as the agency of mediation/mediatization, sustains the subject's desire, while simultaneously acting as the agent of prohibition that prevents its direct, full gratification. (TF, 113)

In other words, my reading suggests that Oedipus can be read as a screen name of sorts (or a 'pinch hitter,' in baseball slang), denoting the overdetermined Freudian subject not only of 'posthuman' cyberspace, but of any human space, which is always an effect of relation or locus.

Oedipus as pinch-hitter

Now my own insistence on the importance of the third in the subjectivizing configuration rests directly on Freud's work, including the founding myth of society that he proposes in *Totem and Taboo*. (After killing the father, the rebellious upstart sons of the tribe finally renounce incestuous gratification and focus their desires beyond the immediate community itself, instituting exogamy, *in response to* the Law that honours the *Dead* Father, who as a posthumous obstacle or ghostly legislator, is the ultimate alien or outsider.) It is not a question of taking this parable literally, but *Totem and Taboo* in fact does suggest how temptation to tragic conflict goes far beyond the conflict of sexual interest in the individual family (the 'Oedipus *complex*'), addressing the even more fundamental human temptation to appropriation and 'theft' of the Other's 'base'. (The high stakes of this dynamic are as true now as they ever were, if one can judge by the year 2000 American presidential election.)

Lacan picks up on this, when he locates the humanizing and social-izing function of the symbolic order as the domain not just of contested and regulated sexuality, but of language itself, the founding of human life. But as early as 1905, Freud's work on jokes already entertainingly emphasized both of these functions — the social configuration and the symbolic function of language — as attributes of *thirdness* in joking. (Freud: 'The tendentious joke calls for *three people* ... when the first person finds his libidinal impulse inhibited by the woman, he develops a hostile trend against the second person [the woman, here], and calls upon the original interfering third party as his ally' [*SE* 8, 100].) In this triangulation, interference deflects an original biological urge into a social circuit, a transactional field potentially distributed among any number of onlooking Others (the joker's audience). And the joking/oedipal triangle always functions as if it had four terms, since it is always picked up and begun anew from home base, in a reiterated circuit which is both compulsive and deflective in nature.[8] Later, in *Beyond the Pleasure Principle*, it is child's play that provides a new example of this mechanism of iteration or 'repetition,' effecting the transformation of a real harrowing situation — the departure of the mother — into a creative kind of solution (the famous *fort-da* game where the toy stands in for the missing object of desire).

The persistence of this modality (opening from imploded dyad to social circuit) insists *throughout* Freud's work, and in fact appears much earlier in Freud's joking scenario than in his work on 'Oedipus proper'. So the priority of what Žižek calls the Oedipus *complex*, as the fundamental structure in psychoanalysis, is open to question. Even if Oedipus as complex provides one particularly compelling narrative instance of a more fundamental intersubjective paradigm, it must be considered (as Lacan points out in his own critique of 'Oedipus proper' in Seminar XV) historically contingent and culturally bound, pitched from the base of European patriarchal culture, the base *from which Freud* himself was theorizing.

In my own relay of these ideas, pitched back at Freud from the new century, I want to insist that Oedipus is less about any formal structure, or any move to save 'Oedipus by other means,' as Žižek claims, than it is about site or differential position itself. My reading is less about complex than *complexity*, in the twenty-first century inflection of that term. For current complexity theory examines the non-linear dynamics of change at the 'tipping-point,' by the addition of a term which changes the very *nature* of the process in which it intervenes (as in mathematics and astronomy, where the 'third body problem' makes the orbit of three interacting bodies impossible to predict, chaotic).

Touching Base, or 'Traversing the Fantasy'

Žižek does point out the importance of 'the intervening Third' (115) in my argument. And I largely concur with his succinct and eloquent formulation of Oedipus' 'view from third': 'In other words, what is 'beyond Oedipus (as a certain historically specified narrative/myth) is Oedipus *itself qua* purely formal structure cosubstantial with the very fact of the symbolic order' (115). Still, Žižek objects to my argument on (appropriately enough) *three* grounds.

1) Žižek claims that 'Oedipus On-line' inadequately explains the persistence of the myth that it claims to replace ('However clear and elucidating it may appear, this difference between Oedipus *qua* mythical narrative and Oedipus *qua* formal structure leaves a crucial question unanswered: where does the need for the narrative supplement to the formal structure come from?' [115]).

2) He objects that a distillation of the oedipal structure eliminates the 'little piece of the real' upon which any symbolic transaction must be based, or it risks hardening into a hollow formalism, lacking mooring in reality (the transference must be supported by the *peu de réel*, by some remainder of the Real' [115]).

3) He concludes that 'Oedipus On-line' hystericizes the subject, in a neuroticization effected by a hyper-repressive symbolic, which even risks provoking psychosis ('Paradoxically, cyberspace thus designates a potential 'relapse' into psychosis, a breakdown of the symbolic mediation, precisely in so far as it actualizes the pure structure of symbolic prohibition/mediation without the 'little piece of the real' of a figure of the father that gives body to it' [115]).

Since Žižek himself suggests that understanding the argument of 'Oedipus On-line' depends on 'getting the break with 'Oedipus proper' clear' (114), I want to touch base with him on these three objections, before heading home:

1) Rather than attempting to promote Oedipus as a strictly symbolic function, limited to pure structure without connection to the real, I suggest that the many different cultural registers in which Freud himself, and then Lacan, replays the narrative versions of the intersubjective circuit, actually enrich its connections with 'real life'. And if anything, cyberspace brings materiality into the symbolic/oedipal equation in a critical way, by making the computer itself—hardware and software—an important player in the interactive intersubjective process.

2) The automatic hystericization of the subject by primal repression — which Žižek claims is reinforced by 'a continuation of Oedipus' — is a Lacanian principle about which I in fact have some real reservations, since Lacan equates the hysteric's discourse with that of the 'barred subject,' without sufficiently distinguishing between the clinical 'pathology' of neurosis and the ontological and epistemological status of the subject as 's/he' who will never know everything, from all positions, at once.

But more important perhaps are the consequences of this skewing, insisting on the hyper-repressive symbolic, for Žižek's own argument. For he suggests that the 'real Father' be reinserted into the oedipal/symbolic formula as a kind of buffer against the symbolic Father, 'a monstrous pure symbolic function, all-devouring and real in his very spectral invisibility' (116). This argument is clearly counter to the insistence of Lacan, and even Freud, concerning the difference between the symbolic father and the real father of experience. But more troubling is the reason cited to justify the necessary replacement of the symbolic paternal function with a flesh-and-blood representative. For Žižek repeatedly reveals a temptation to do away with the figure of the father altogether, symbolic or 'real,' framed in a rhetorical question which actually seems to cloak a desire to escape the circuit of Law itself: 'Why can the formal structure not reign in its purity, without its confusing identification with an empirical 'pathological' element (the paternal figure) that gives body to it?' (115).

One answer to this question would be that the symbolic can and does function in countless instances without being embodied by a flesh-and-blood father, as Freud's own examples concerning joking, creative writing, cultural inmixing, and the transference in analysis attest. But Žižek continues: 'why can we not simply enter the symbolic order, and directly assume the loss involved in this entry?'. The framing of this strange rhetorical query, while acknowledging the impossibility of this 'direct entry,' none the less manifests a longing for 'simplicity' and 'directness' which is the antithesis of the symbolic move. Indeed, the entry into the symbolic is essentially and inherently a process of complexification, necessitating a structural long circuiting, and you can't somehow get home by 'directly' traversing the field (or the fantasy) and simply skipping the bases.

Žižek goes on to link his query, however, with the enigma of the prohibition in psychoanalysis. His observation is framed with a rhetoric of assumption that is found throughout the essay, whereby performance substitutes itself for demonstration, sliding into the place of certainty ('it is easy to see'; 'it is needless to add'): 'Needless to add, we thereby encounter the enigma of the prohibition of the impossible; if *jouissance* [the enjoyment of the object of desire] is impossible, why do we need the gesture of formally prohibiting it?' (115). Again, Freud might answer that it is not a question here of a legal move, or a voluntaristic or conscious *gesture*, or even of what we *need*; but of unconscious, and even primal, repression, a structural prohibition inhering in the configuration and the nature of human desire itself.

But more specifically, Žižek seems puzzled about what he sees as the central enigma: the prohibition or law (the incest taboo laid down by the symbolic father) seems 'superfluous,' since enjoyment (*jouissance*) is 'always already' impossible. But this circular reasoning suffers from another elision, another short-circuit: it conflates the symbolic register with the 'real world'. For of course *real* incestuous 'enjoyment' is in no way physically impossible or unheard of in the real world — witness the countless cases of child seduction and rape within the family. However, the very base of the psychoanalytic endeavour is the discovery of the radical incommensurability of our psychic desire with its 'real life' objects: *even when* desire is consummated, our objects always give us chase, staying one step ahead of us. It is in the nature of human desire not to coincide adequately with its objects, always missing the appointment on base (quite simply, we want what we don't have, and when we have something, we displace our desire on to something else). To my mind, the only adequate explanation for this perversity of desire is given by Freud in *The Three Theories of Sexuality (1905)*, when he suggests that in its very nature and structure, human desire is always off-track and out of line, pursuing something always already lost, and is thus always already misplaced and replaced onto substitute objects with which it does not fully coincide.

But Žižek, brilliant theorist that he is, of course knows all this, and in fact elaborates on this dynamic of deflection and skewing throughout his work. But like every theorist, or every referee, he seems to be suffering an eclipse in his vision and in his reasoning, stemming, presumably, from his own stake in arguing against what he in fact, 'as a Lacanian philosopher,' already knows.

What are these personal stakes? I cannot presume to speculate, from my own limited vantage-point, but I can point out the effects of Žižek's blind spot on his theory — he ends up suggesting that the real father *must* be a player in the symbolic act of subject-formation. And why? To *avoid* the consequences of the symbolic act, by sidestepping them, allowing illusion and fantasy to persist:

So the only consistent answer to the question: 'Why does the superfluous prohibition emerge, which merely prohibits the impossible?' is: in order to obfuscate this inherent possibility — that is, in order to sustain the illusion that, were it not for the externally imposed prohibition, the full gratification would be possible. (166)

In other words, Žižek is positing 'fetishism' and disavowal here as the fundamental operation in subject-formation, and as a fundamental alibi for foreclosing a devouring Father too terrible to be faced, a symbolic debt (to use Lacan's term) too heavy to be assumed. Or in more general terms, Žižek seems to be suggesting that it is perhaps the truth of death or inadequacy which the subject must elude at all costs, hope against hope: maybe *I* can avoid the lesson of Oedipus, maybe *I* can have my cake and eat it too (or, in the masculinist language of fetishism) maybe 'mother' really *does* have 'my' genitalia, maybe *I* myself am not subject to any kind of wounding . . . maybe the oracle does not really apply to *me*.

Žižek ends up disqualifying 'Oedipus On-line' on the strange grounds that it does not postulate this escape — in other words, that it fails to provide an alibi, a denial or disavowal of the symbolic order itself:

The problem with 'Oedipus on-line' is thus that what is missing in it is precisely this 'pacifying' function of the paternal figure which enables us to obfuscate the debilitating deadlock of desire. (115, my emphasis)

Indeed. 'Oedipus On-line' does decline to position not only cyber-life, but all aspects of human life, in Eden rather than at the crossroads between Corinth and Thebes.

And while my point *is* indeed that cyberspace does not provide immersion or escape — which Žižek himself has labelled as 'psychotic' — but that it still is governed by the rules of human symbolic interaction, I would not call this a *problem*. Or rather, the problem that seems to plague Žižek here inheres in the human condition itself, whereby nothing may be gained in a short-circuit that wants to 'steal the very base' of human subjectivity, the implication of the Other as a position or function that will not just go away, an Other that *simultaneously* defers and enables 'my' actions. Unlike the idiosyncratic 'father' of Žižek's fable, the Other does not elide or obscure difficulty in order to pacify me with an illusory solution — and, thankfully, the Other that we call 'Oedipus,' a screen name for the structure of complexity or thirdness, will not simply 'sign off' in order to allow us to steal home.

Another symptom of this phantasm in Žižek's own position is perhaps his equation of 'perversity' not with the free circulation of 'polymorphous perverse' libido, but with male masochism, which for him actually obfuscates a longing for discipline at the hands of the dominatrix (the 'phallic mother' of 'Slaves are Us,' the New York agency cited in Žižek's own strange double play [118]). In any case, Žižek plays doubly double — his private fantasy eliminating a terrible symbolic father is in fact reinforced by a 'need' for the 'pacifying' 'real father,' who seems to have some traditional 'maternal' qualities; on the other hand, the fantasy of an infantile reunion with the mother that subtends the formulation of 'parent-as-pacifier' seems to be accompanied by a 'need' for a 'chastizing' 'real Mother' (the dominatrix). This cross-dressing at the oedipal crossroads seems at once to mask, regender, and reconfigure the terrifying Symbolic Father as Phallic Mother, and the nurturing mother as pacifying father, in order to avoid the confrontation (at the Oedipal intersection or website) with the other as . . . ineluctably Other.

3) Finally, as the above example should make clear, my own reading of Oedipus does not in any way disqualify the mythic resonance of Oedipus, in favour of an empty symbolic structure. My reading does de-emphasise the Father as personality rather than position, by suggesting that the family romance is not the only important aspect of the myth of Oedipus. For the myth of Oedipus is just as much about the vicissitudes of knowledge as about any rivalry or usurpation of erotic rights: as Oedipus solves the riddle of the Sphinx, he becomes the Subject Supposed to Know, implicated in the imploded short-circuit (the marriage with Jocasta is his deadly reward for presuming to know all). And Lacan's replay of Oedipus as the 'symbolic order' foregrounds this aspect.

Indeed, in Seminar XV, Lacan emphasizes the *failure* of analysis, as the fall of the Subject Supposed to Know, a move which exposes the analyst as a mere mortal implicated in the countertransference. Just so, the tragic history of Oedipus is one of misrecognition, based on the fact that his knowledge is not so much profound as clever (he is good at riddles), intrepid but empty (as he searches for the culprit), and blind in the crucial spot where the criminal himself 'looks back' from his own mirror. 'Oedipus On-line' does not neglect the myth, but it seeks to dislocate the privilege and priority of 'Oedipus the King' — a coronation that has contributed to so many misunderstandings and reductions of Freud (as 'only about sex').

In fact Žižek's own most compelling theorizations of the subject in culture, based on pointing out the blind spot in any field of vision, are strikingly demonstrated by the drama of misrecognition and discovery, blindness and insight, that Oedipus enacts — as Greek monarch, player, and now, internaut, navigating the field of digital interaction.

Coming Home, or Traversing the Fantasy as Short-Circuit

In his concluding move, after pathologizing all three positions he treats (as psychotic, perverse, and neurotic, respectively), Žižek performs a kind of 'goldilocks play':

> That is to say, both standard reactions to cyberspace are deficient: one is 'too strong' (cyberspace as involving a break with Oedipus); one is 'too weak' (cyberspace as a continuation of Oedipus by other means) (116–117).

This move collapses the original triad, citing only two positions (the first is too hard, the second is too soft), leaving his own position (which would seem to be 'just right') to stand in at third. But his position is actually a replay of Turkle and Stone's 'perverse' position, corrected from Žižek's own point of view (the 'perverse' view is acceptable, he tells us, 'on condition that one characterizes perversion *in a much stricter* way' [116]. Thus Žižek's own final disciplinary action as referee reverses the disciplinary scenario of the male masochist and the bitch goddess in this already confusing mix, conflating the position of object and Other ('the proverbial male masochist elevates his partner into a Law-giver whose orders are to be obeyed' (...) [thus] 'it is the object itself that makes the law,' with the perverse process henceforth 'locating enjoyment in the very agency that prohibits access to enjoyment' (117). (The player desires the umpire? Then he cannot be keeping his eye on the ball, which is the only way to score.)

In any case, after this conflation of positions, Žižek again multiplies them; for in the very next passage he reinstates *four* positions, but reorders them, switching second and third, in a kind of shell game that may also suggest a kind of skill at 'hypnotizing' his audience by his verbal agility. But this time he at least seems to propose a conciliation among the four positions, instead of holding out for a declared winner ('What if it is wrong and misleading to ask directly which of the four versions of the libidinal/symbolic economy that we outlined — the psychotic suspension of the Oedipus complex, the continuation of the Oedipus complex by other means, the perverse staging of the Law, traversing the fantasy — is the correct one?' [123]). Yet in renaming the players in a reshuffled line-up, Žižek has perhaps pitched yet another slider. For he has sneaked the "Oedipus *complex*' back into the game in the final play, embedded in the very position ('the continuation of the Oedipus *complex* by other means') which he previously pointedly characterized as empty of content/complex, as pure structure without narrative.

But the bigger problem is perhaps that a 'fantasy of the fantasy' subtends Žižek's conclusion. The 'fundamental fantasy' that cyberspace is supposed to traverse is conceived as a scene so terrible and ineffable that it can never be formulated or confronted, and yet, Žižek depicts it here, quite graphically, as a region where dislocated limbs float around — where the *disjecta membra*, veiled in the Latin phrase, suggest a displaced fantasy of castration. And how are we supposed to traverse this scene, which we can never actually confront? By 'acting out' in cyberspace: 'And perhaps cyberspace, with its capacity to externalize our innermost fantasies in all their inconsistency, opens up to artistic practice a unique possibility to stage, to 'act out,' the fantasmatic support of our existence, up to the fundamental 'sado-masochistic' fantasy that can never be subjectivized' (122).

However, as Freud and Lacan certainly were at pains to point out, 'acting out' is the antithesis of 'working through'. And the 'fundamental fantasy,' unassimilable to the subject here, in fact seems to stage a veiled replay of Žižek's 'perverse' scene (the male masochist suffering humiliation and dismemberment at the hands of 'the Lady of the House'.) Indeed, Žižek's prescription for traversing the fantasy, and thus 'working-through' its symptoms (possible only 'if we follow [cyberspace] to the end, if we immerse ourselves in it without restraint' [122-3]) sounds suspiciously like the original regressive 'illness' itself, the 'first base position' which Žižek characterized earlier as 'the dystopian prospect of individuals regressing to pre-symbolic psychotic immersion' (111). Žižek's 'post-oedipal' trajectory sends him back to first base, without scoring his final point.

Perhaps it would be better to readmit Oedipus to the game.

None the less Žižek's concluding move, which proposes to reopen the question of the social and material contexts and consequences of cyber-subjectivity, is one that is well worth cheering on.

What if, ultimately [. . .] the choice is ours, the stake in a politico-ideological struggle? How cyberspace will affect us is not directly inscribed into its technological properties, *it hinges on the network of socio-symbolic relations* (of power and domination, etc) which always-already overdetermine the way cyberspace affects us. (123, my emphasis)

These are certainly words to 'play' by. However, since it is precisely just such a 'network of socio-symbolic relations' that Freud and Lacan were at pains to configure in and as the oedipal/symbolic register, Žižek's very conclusion would seem to put Oedipus back in circulation.

Perhaps it is best to consign the postgame wrap-up to the players of popular culture. The good news is that in 'Who's on First,' Costello does finally manage to understand Abbott's pitch. But even this momentary base of knowledge, where Costello reels off information in the rapid-fire delivery of the sportscaster, is immediately resituated between certainty and uncertainty, *'stopped short'* — and sent back around to visit all the bases — by the intervention of the Other.

Costello: Who picks up the ball and throws it to What. What throws it to I Don't Know. I Don't Know throws it back to Tomorrow, triple play! Another guy gets up and hits a long fly ball to Because. Why? I Don't Know! He's on third and . . . I DON'T GIVE A DARN!
Abbott: Oh . . . that's our shortstop.

As a player in the intersubjective field, Oedipus comes to know all too well that feigned indifference or innocence will not suffice to get us out of the game. It just 'stops us short,' puts us back on base, and on-line.

JERRY ALINE FLIEGER
Rutgers University

NOTES

1   Abbott and Costello, 'Who's On First?' (1936), cited from the Internet site *IMDB.com*. The recorded text may also be heard at this site.
2   The schema L and the symbolic order are discussed at some length in Anthony Wilden's *The Language of the Self* (Baltimore, Johns Hopkins University Press, 1984), 270–86. Wilden's piece is based on Lacan's *Champ et fonction du langage dans la psychanalyse, Écrits* I (Paris, Editions du Seuil, 1971).
3   Slavoj Žižek, *The Plague of Fantasies* (New York and London, Verso, 1997).
4   Slavoj Žižek, 'Is it Possible to Traverse the Fantasy in Cyberspace?,' *The Žižek Reader*, eds. Elizabeth Wright and Edmond Wright (Oxford, Blackwell Publishers, 1999), 102–24.

5 See, for instance, *The Purloined Punch Line: Freud's Comic Theory and the Postmodern Text* (Baltimore, Johns Hopkins University Press, 1990); 'The Listening Eye: Postmodernism, Paranoia, and the Hyper-Visible' (*Diacritics*, 26:1 1996); and more recently, 'Overdetermined Oedipus: Mommy, Daddy, and Me as Desiring Machine,' *South Atlantic Quarterly*, 96:3 (Summer 1997); reprinted in *A Deleuzian Century?*, ed. Ian Buchanan (Raleigh, North Carolina, Duke University Press, 2000). See also 'Deleuze, Feminism, and the Molecular Unconscious,' in *Deleuze and Feminist Theory*, eds. Ian Buchanan and Claire Colebrook (Edinburgh University Press, 2000).
6 'Is Oedipus On-line?' 91; see also my article in *Diacritics* 26 (1996), noted above.
7 Allucquére Rosanne Stone, *The War of Desire and Technology at the Close of the Mechanical Age* (Cambridge, Massachusetts, MIT Press, 1995). See especially Chapter 8: 'Conclusion: The Gaze of the Vampire'.

'There is no Other of the Other' Symptoms of a Decline in Symbolic Faith, or, Žižek's Anti-capitalism

> The premiss of the series is that the explosive combination of Lacanian psycho-analysis and Marxist tradition detonates a dynamic freedom that enables us to question the very presuppositions of the circuit of Capital.[1]

So ends the 1994 policy statement of Slavoj Žižek's *Wo Es War* series with Verso. For all his forays into German idealism and cultural studies, this clarion call makes explicit Žižek's central preoccupation with Lacanian psychoanalysis and Marxism, stretching back to at least the very beginning of his prodigious scholarly output in the English language. It may strike us as a bit curious, then, that those scholars for whom Žižek serves as inspiration for social and political analysis have chosen to focus on his Lacanian interventions in multicultural, social movement, and sex debates, silently relegating his Marxism to a secondary and incoherent remnant of an outdated leftist project.

In this essay, I wish to begin redressing this balance by system-atically gathering together a selection of relevant passages dispersed throughout his oeuvre. My aim is to offer up for scrutiny one possible account of the relation between Žižek's Lacanian psychoanalysis and Marxism — one which avoids reducing it to a pragmatic cobbling together of two otherwise distinct tools which he would seem to deploy indiscriminately in an attack upon capitalism.

The Subject as Ethical

Subjectivity and ethics. It is with these concepts that I propose to show how Žižek's Lacanian psychoanalysis and Marxism share a deep structural homology that belies an otherwise superficial and opportunistic link to anti-capitalism. Relying upon this homology, Žižek effectively argues that the discourse of capitalism promotes a certain kind of subjectivity[2] that corresponds to what he calls an ethics of desire.

Put simply, my argument is that implicit in Žižek's anti-capitalism is an ethical critique which is animated by Marx's analyses of political economy and made possible by Lacan's ethics of psychoanalysis. Following Lacan, he suggests the counterintuitive and unsettling possibility of penetrating directly through desire, coming out on the as yet unexplored side of drive. (More of this later.) Without this move, Žižek suggests that political philosophy's current appeals to communicative ideals, rational or moral deliberation, and openness to the otherness of the Other, will remain impotent in the face of a growing number of newly emerging social symptoms (fundamentalist extremisms, racist outbursts, nationalist warring, or the perceived omnipresent threats posed by immigrants, hooligans, animal rights terrorists, paedophiles, etc.).

Of course, Žižek agrees with Marx that capitalism has ushered in a new realm of freedom unknown to premodern times. He agrees that by running roughshod over traditional forms of life, the logic of capital has succeeded in dissolving the superstitious and theological foundations of traditional forms of official authority and prejudice, pitilessly tearing 'asunder the motley feudal ties that bound man to his 'natural superiors''.[3] As Marx and Engels famously put it, '[a]ll fixed, fast-frozen relations, with their train of ancient and venerable prejudices and opinions, are swept away, all new-formed ones become antiquated before they can ossify. All that is solid melts into air'.[4]

But Žižek's central concern is with the counterintuitive conse-quences of living in a society that is more liberal and permissive than ever before. Contrary to what we would expect, the disintegration of traditional forms of authority, does not lead to a healthy burgeoning of pleasurable experiences. Quite the contrary, it leads to forms of even greater oppression. In this view, there is such a thing as power without authority and this, it is argued, is far more stifling than the type of power associated with traditional forms of control. In Lacanian terms, this disintegration of traditional forms of authority coincides with the decline of our faith in the symbolic Other (the symbolic order).

By linking the logic of capital to the ethics of desire, Žižek's psychoanalytic approach to social analysis is meant to explain what might otherwise appear to contradict our commonsense intuitions, and to demonstrate how contemporary subjectivity is ethically impli-cated, rather than the mere plaything of an inevitable and inexorable expansion of the capitalist discourse. In summary, my reconstruction of Žižek's argument involves giving an account of his conception of capitalism and its impact upon the traditional notion of trust or symbolic faith; an account of Žižek's unease with much contemporary theorizing of political subjectivity; an account of the fantasmatic logic of desire and how this can be linked to the logic of capitalism; an outline of the rationale underpinning what Žižek takes to be the social symptoms of a decline in symbolic faith; a more concerted attempt to highlight the central ingredients constituting the social fantasies of capitalism; and finally, a consideration of some theoretical and strategic implications regarding the problem of intervention in concrete political life.

Capitalism . . .

'Constant revolutionizing of production, uninterrupted disturbance of all social conditions, everlasting uncertainty and agitation distinguish the bourgeois epoch from all earlier ones'.[5] Thus goes one of Marx's formulations of the capitalist stage of history. While capitalism as an historical epoch shares with previous historical modes of production the notion that class struggle is defined in terms of who owns the means of production, capitalism is most clearly differentiated from other forms of socio-economic organization by the fact that its mode of production is characterized by its inherent imbalance, its tendency to overthrow itself. In this view, owners of capital increase their investment returns primarily on the basis of expanding their market share and by driving down labour wages to subsistence levels, thereby threatening its very own survival and forcing a revolution in its mode of operation. Thus, for Žižek, '[t]he elementary feature of capitalism consists of its inherent structural imbalance, its innermost antagonistic character: the constant crisis, the constant revolutionizing of its conditions of existence'.[6] Now, more than ever, 'he suggests, 'one should reassert Marx's old formula that the limit of capitalism is Capital itself'.[7]

The important thing to highlight here is the idea that the logic of capitalism is characterized by *an internal-structural, not empirical, limit*. Despite some expressed reservations,[8] Žižek hints in a short footnote[9] that his contemporary articulation of the Marxist concept of capitalism comes very close to that offered by Hardt and Negri in their *Empire*.[10] For they too underline the restive character of capitalism, pointing to Marx's comment that '[t]he tendency to create the world market is directly given in the concept of capital itself. Every limit appears as a barrier to be overcome'.[11] But, Hardt and Negri insist, this theoretical limit, whose concrete manifestation takes the form of recurrent crises, does not function as a negative force. Capital's limit is a paradoxical limit in the sense that it is a positive and *productive* limit. As they put it, 'crisis is for capital a *normal* condition that indicates not its end but its tendency and *mode of operation*'.[12] This limit, then, is its ontological condition of possibility, not its ultimate fatal flaw. Empirically, capital 'is an organism that cannot sustain itself without constantly looking beyond its boundaries, feeding off its external environment'. Ontologically, however, outside barriers are *constitutive*. As Hardt and Negri put it, capital's 'outside is *essential*'.[13] In this view, therefore, capitalism's contradictions are productive contradictions: 'capital's reliance on its outside, on the non-capitalist environment, which satisfies the need to realize surplus value, conflicts with the internalization of the noncapitalist environment, which satisfies the need to capitalize that realized surplus value.... [Thus] [c]apital's thirst must be quenched with new blood, and it must continually seek new frontiers'.[14]

A final, crucial, point is how this logic is independent of the particular socio-cultural characteristics of the non-capitalist domains its seeks to internalize. In other words, the different domains of capital are united not on the basis of the positive characteristics they share: 'capital does not really make noncapitalist territories 'after its own image,' as if all were becoming homogeneous'.[15] Capital in fact *respects* cultural difference, it *acknowledges* the specificity of the Other. When a corporation moves into Asia or Eastern Europe, it quenches its thirst for surplus value by taking into account the specificity of socio-cultural mores, whether in terms of working practices or in terms of consumer expectations.[16] It is precisely because the logic of capital is *empty* of positive content, that it can be set to work *immanently*: it erodes traditions from *within*, so to speak. As Hardt and Negri put it, '[e]ach segment of the noncapitalist environment is transformed differently, and all are integrated organically into the expanding body of capital. In other words, the different segments of the outside are internalized not on the model of similitude but as different organs that function together in one coherent body'.[17]

. . . and its Impact upon Symbolic Faith in Symbolic Other

As I have already suggested, one central consequence of the expansion of capitalism's reach into wider and wider areas of social life, is the putting into question of relations premised upon our faith in traditional figures of authority and associated relations of subordination. It has the effect of *politicizing* traditionally disadvantaged subject positions linked to sex, race, age, social status, culture, nation, etc.[18] In other words, it has the effect of bringing to the fore the contingency underlying supposedly necessary and naturally sedimented identities. This point has been highlighted by Ernesto Laclau, for whom this radical politicization, this visibility of contingency, 'is directly linked to the level and extension of structural dislocations operating in contemporary capitalism'.[19] In this sense, of course, capitalism acts as liberator. It dissolves traditional social relations, thereby creating the conditions for the creation of new identities. That it sees in these new identities and relations only the potential for new profitable markets should not obscure this central fact.

But the outcome of this relentless dissolution of traditional hierarchies has also been a general doubting of symbolic authority *as such*. This, it is claimed, is structurally connected to a whole series of social symptoms which contemporary normative political theory has linked to the decline of trust (or so-called social capital) in liberal-democratic societies.[20] These symptoms cover a wide spectrum — from the perceived rise of fundamentalisms and racist intolerance, cynicism and voter apathy, mob hysteria vis-à-vis immigrants and paedophiles, the popularity of conspiracy theories, the fascination with chance games that promise heavenly monetary rewards (while the poor flock to lottery and betting agencies, the rich splurge in posh casinos and play the stock market), so-called postmodern 'trash' art, retreats to the real of nature (in an attempt to recoup certainty in the various General Theories of Everything, in the complete objectification of the human in the form of a genome map, in the Spiritual Balance of Eastern Mysticism), to postmodern theories of multiculturalism.

In order to appreciate how Žižek links such a disparate set of symptoms, it is important to note that for him what sets the stage for traditional (modern) authority is Judaeo-Christian religion. According to Žižek, the substitution of monotheism for polytheism signaled the start of an irreversible shift in the social subject's modality that made possible the emergence of modernity. In this view, it was God's prohibition that dissolved the old sexualized Wisdom, making space for non-sexualized abstract knowledge: '[T]here is "objective" scientific knowledge (in the modern, post-Cartesian sense of the term) only if the universe of scientific knowledge itself is supplemented and sustained' by a prohibitory paternal figure, by a 'God of groundless Willing and ferocious irrational rage'.[21]

The moment the central reference point sustaining the symbolic Other becomes unstuck, the moment, for example, our monotheistic God *qua* prohibitory figure (and all its substitutable equivalents, ranging from the King, the Father, the President, the Judge, to the Scientist) recedes, a whole series of social symptoms emerge in an attempt by the social subject to regain its balance. This may appear in the form of a return to 'the Jungian neo-obscurantist notion of the masculine and feminine eternal archetypes which thrives today,'[22] or it may appear in the form of a kind of

sprouting of 'committees' destined to decide upon the so-called ethical dilemmas which crop up when technological developments ever-increasingly affect our life-world: not only cyberspace but also domains as diverse as medicine and biogenetics on the one hand, and the rules of sexual conduct and the protection of human rights on the other, confront us with the need to invent the basic rules of proper ethical conduct, since we lack any form of big Other, any symbolic point of reference that would serve as a safe and unproblematic moral anchor.[23]

In this latter case, Žižek suggests that 'these (re)invented rules supplant the lack of a fundamental Law/Prohibition (. . .) It is as if the lack of the big Other is supplanted by "ethical committees" as so many substitute "small big Others" on to which the subject transposes his responsibility and from which he expects to receive a formula that will resolve his deadlock'.[24]

The implicit suggestion here is that the expansion of capitalism has resulted in a thoroughgoing reflexivization of society wherein subjects no longer can rely on stable symbolic references. Now, 'there is no Nature or Tradition providing a firm foundation on which one can rely, [so that] even our innermost impetuses (sexual orientation, etc.) are more and more experienced as something to be chosen. How to feed and educate a child, how to proceed in sexual seduction, how and what to eat, how to relax and amuse oneself—all these spheres are increasingly "colonized" by reflexivity, that is, experienced as something to be learned and decided upon'.[25] In this view, 'all the expert government panels and ethical committees, and so on, are there to conceal [the] radical openness and uncertainty' of being forced to take decisions without a proper foundation in knowledge.[26]

So, what kind of subjectivity characterizes this capitalism-induced super-reflexivity; and what kind of ethical stances does it make possible? Though these two questions will be tackled directly later in this essay, it is worth pointing out how this double inquiry parallels Žižek's critique of 'risk society' theorists. This is because Žižek feels that whilst risk theorists have accurately grasped the increased uncertainty associated with the requirement that more and more decisions be made in the face of low probability, high consequence dilemmas, they have not only misconstrued the source of this new, highly reflexive experience (i.e., the logic of capitalism), but have also underestimated its impact upon modern subjectivity and therefore upon our ethical horizon. According to Žižek, 'today we are witnessing a shift no less radical than the shift from the pre-modern patriarchal order directly legitimized by the sexualized cosmology (Masculine and Feminine as the two cosmic principles) to the modern patriarchal order that introduced the abstract-universal notion of man'.[27] Thus, though risk theorists have correctly punctured the naive certainties of the first wave of modernization, they have not moved sufficiently beyond standard variations of dominant conceptions of the modern subject 'able to reason and reflect freely, to decide on and select his/her set of norms, and so on'.[28]

Without an adequate conception of today's subjectivity, Žižek claims, risk theorists not only are powerless to explain the rise of anxiety associated with greater choice and with increased access to information, but are also unable to offer plausible ways forward. As we have already seen, the rise in number of ethical committees is a false solution to the problem. Indeed it is simply a symptom that is part of the problem. So too, for that matter, is a whole new layer of service industries designed to help subjects cope with the overabundance of choices by delimiting and packaging them on the basis of pre-agreed customer profiles.

From a psychoanalytic point of view, this rise in anxiety coincides with the undermining of our symbolic faith in the big Other which, in turn, is a direct consequence of today's panreflexivity. The more we put into question institutionally-sedimented dictates, thereby making more and more dimensions of our identity a matter of individual choice, the more any remaining authoritative impositions must be legitimized by means of our individually expressed consent. And this consent, in turn, is given largely on a contractual basis that suggests that those in positions of authority will no longer be trusted at face value, but will be judged on their capacity to meet our expectations, to satisfy precisely specified — preferably measurable — objectives.

Notions like trust and loyalty are therefore a natural casualty in a pan-reflexive world. This is because 'trust always involves a leap of faith' that cannot be reduced to rational deliberation. As Žižek puts it, '[t]o say "I trust you because I have decided, upon rational reflection, to trust you" involves the same paradox as the statement

"Having weighed up the reasons for and against, I decided to obey my father"'.[29] Today, however, this is precisely how trust and loyalty are being understood. Think, for example, of concepts like brand loyalty (which targets consumers) and company loyalty (which targets workers). These terms seem to appeal to a traditional conception of trust requiring a symbolic leap of faith. Nowadays, however, consumer loyalty is as capricious and ephemeral as is market demand and the potential for profit. Similarly, calls to greater labour adaptability, efficiency, transferability, and flexibility directly undermine the very conditions for employer-employee fidelity. Today's time-scales are simply not conducive to earning respect and are thus more susceptible to its being bought (through so-called 'golden' hellos and 'golden' handcuffs). As Richard Sennett puts it, '[d]elayed gratification loses its value (. . .) in a regime whose institutions change rapidly; it becomes absurd to work long and hard for an employer who thinks only about selling and moving on'.[30] It is the increasing prevalence of this kind of loyalty that creates the conditions for an increasingly litigious society, and a kind of politics that relies more and more on commercial market research tools, like opinion polls and focus groups.

Postmodernism, Identity, Subjectivity

As we have seen, what characterizes the logic of capital most succinctly for Žižek is its emptiness, its internal yet productive limit, its structurally 'open' character that makes it such a formidable force in eroding traditional and modern relations of subordination. It should be obvious by now, therefore, why he perceives a latent danger in contemporary leftist projects of emancipation that come to rely too exclusively upon postmodern and postcolonial theories of identity. Žižek, for example, warns that 'the elated 'deconstructionist' logomachy focused on 'essentialism' and 'fixed identities' ultimately fights a straw-man. Far from containing any kind of subversive potentials, the dispersed, plural, constructed subject hailed by postmodern theory . . . simply designates *the form of subjectivity that corresponds to late capitalism*'.[31] As Hardt and Negri put it,

[w]hen we begin to consider the ideologies of corporate capital and the world market, it certainly appears that the postmodernist and postcolonialist theorists who advocate a politics of difference, fluidity, and hybridity in order to challenge the binaries and essentialism of modern sovereignty have been outflanked by the

strategies of power … These theorists thus find themselves pushing against an open door … This new enemy not only is not resistant to the old weapons but actually thrives on them, and thus joins its would-be antagonists in applying them to the fullest. Long live difference! Down with essentialist binaries![32]

Their fear, then, is that the values of anti-essentialism, contingency, and irony (along with a related set comprising undecidability, uncertainty, risk, hybridity, fluidity, diversity, sensitivity to context, etc.) are the values that the current ideology of corporate capital celebrate.[33]

What, then, it might be asked, can contemporary critical theory legitimately hope to achieve? Even if we accept that capital has undisputed corrosive effects, is it sufficient to simply point this out? Is it sufficient for the Left to make explicit its empty, albeit dynamic, logic, revealing it as our new and powerful enemy? If we were to leave the critique of capitalism at this level, however, Žižek would scarcely have moved the debate beyond the standard analytical distinction between objective scientific knowledge (of the actual workings of capital) and (capitalist) ideology.[34] This, after all, is why Hardt and Negri claim that theories 'that privilege the pure critique of the dynamics of capital risk undervaluing the power of the real efficient motor that drives capitalist development from its deepest core: the movements and struggles of the proletariat'.[35] Such analyses 'will not be sufficient here because in the end they stop at the threshold of the analysis of subjectivity and concentrate rather on the contradictions of capital's own development'. In their view, '[h]istory has a logic only when subjectivity rules it, only when … the emergence of subjectivity reconfigures efficient causes and final causes in the development of history. The power of the proletariat consists precisely in this'. Thus, they urge, we 'need to identify a theoretical schema that puts the subjectivity of the social movements of the proletariat at centre stage in the process of globalization and the constitution of global order'.[36]

Perhaps we can take this as the central reason why Žižek has recourse to Lacan's theory of subjectivity.

The Logic of Capitalism and its link to the Subject of Desire

It is obvious, Žižek suggests, that a socio-economic order under the sway of profit-motivated market capitalism celebrates 'ruthless competition: individualism'.[37] According to neo-liberal doxa, of course, this is not something to be ashamed of. On the contrary, it is the very motor of our economy, the very source of our unprecedented wealth and economic growth. But it is precisely the type of subjectivity this motor relies on that provides the link between the logic of capital and the Lacanian logic of desire.

The way that Žižek establishes this link is via another Lacanian concept, the *objet petit a*. He argues that there is an

inherent link between three notions: that of Marxist surplus-value, that of the Lacanian *objet petit a* as surplus-enjoyment (the concept that Lacan elaborated with direct reference to Marxian surplus value), and the paradox of the superego, perceived long ago by Freud: the more Coke you drink, the thirstier you are; the more profit you make, the more you want; the more you obey the superego command, the guiltier you are — in all three cases, the logic of balanced exchange is disturbed in favour of an excessive logic (. . .). The key to this disturbance, of course, is the surplus-enjoyment, the *objet petit a*, which exists (or, rather, persists) in a kind of curved space — the nearer you get to it, the more it eludes your grasp.[38]

The suggestion here is that Lacan's logic of desire and the logic of capitalism share a deep homology in structuring contemporary subjectivity.[39] This is because, just as the subject of capitalism is empty, so too is the subject of desire. In both cases, the logics are purely formal and independent of the particular concrete contexts wherein they function. The discourse of capitalism can only have as its main objective the failure to satisfy desire, thereby keeping desire alive, sustaining an insatiable desire for new products, new commodities, thereby leading to a kind of 'fetishism of the new' whose consequence is the ever-expanding frontiers of capitalist market relations.

This excessive logic finds its principle of explanation in the simple nature of desire itself: short of extinguishing the subject *qua* subject of desire, it is imperative that each new object of desire *fail* to satisfy the subject. Ultimately, each object of desire can only be an imaginary lure veiling the substanceless void which actually functions as the cause of desire. This is why it would be appropriate to refer to the *objet petit a* as a *fantasmatic* object: the very survival of the subject as a subject of desire *depends* upon the radical extraction of its ultimate object of desire; it *depends* upon its never being fully satisfied.

Fantasy, then, is a narrative that covers over the necessary dissatis-faction of the subject — its lack ($) — by means of a reference to the *objet petit a* (a), whose primordial extraction supports this lack. It does this by linking our objects of desire to obstacles that prevent their direct consumption, redirecting our desire onto the secret wish to eliminate such obstacles (e.g., wishing the downfall of a successful colleague or the deportation of immigrants, indulging in welfare or financial misdemeanours, etc.).

The peculiar characteristic of this logic of desire involves the impossible task of maintaining a 'proper' distance toward our objects of desire. And yet this is precisely how we procure a sense of *being*, of *jouissance* (libidinal satisfaction or enjoyment). The more distant the object of desire, the more pleasurable our fantasmatic indulgence; the closer we get, the more horrific it becomes. The logic of desire is thus structurally unbalanced and excessive — it can never achieve a 'proper' measure, it is never 'just right': The beatific and the horrific aspects of fantasy are inseparable and mutually constitutive. Of course, this latter, counterintuitive insight, makes sense only against the background of the subject as a subject of desire: in order to sustain itself as such (i.e., as a subject of desire) it must prevent itself from full satisfaction. Otherwise its very being will be at stake, evoking intense anxiety and provoking a whole range of actings-out or 'false acts'.[40] This logic also accounts for a series of symptoms, whose clinical variants range from obsessional cleaning rituals and procrastination to conversion symptoms.

Symptoms of a Decline in Symbolic Faith

So what, precisely, is the benefit of introducing Lacan's theory of subjectivity? In a first approach this psychoanalytic incursion is designed to answer the following question that Žižek poses: 'Why does the decline of paternal authority and fixed social and gender roles generate new anxieties, instead of opening up a Brave New World of individuals engaged in the creative "care of the Self" and enjoying the perpetual process of shifting and reshaping their fluid multiple identities'?[41]

If the dynamic logic of capitalism serves as one of Žižek's central targets, it is because it relies on a certain kind of subjectivity. If, therefore, the critique of political economy is a precondition for the effective critique of contemporary (racial, sexual, environmental, etc.) inequalities it is not because of some sort of substantive causal role that the economy plays, but because of the void-cause it conceals and the empty subjectivity this makes possible. Thus, Žižek's claim that *'the depoliticized economy is the disavowed "fundamental fantasy" of postmodern politics'*[42] is not meant to demonize the 'objective' logic of capitalism within which the subject has no role to play. Quite the contrary. It is precisely the reference to this disavowed fantasy that not only reintroduces the subject into political and ideological analysis, but portrays it as ethically implicated. For this reason, in today's global society, 'a properly political act would necessarily entail the repoliticization of the economy: within a given situation, a gesture counts as an [ethical] *act* only in so far as it disturbs ("traverses") its fundamental fantasy'.[43]

So when Žižek alerts us to the danger linked to the continued expansion of the capitalist logic, this danger is conceived as an inherent danger specific to the subjectivity it relies on, namely, the subject of desire:

> Lacan designated capitalism as the reign of the discourse of the hysteric: this vicious circle of desire, whose apparent satisfaction only widens the gap of its dissatisfaction, is what defines hysteria. A kind of structural homology exists between capitalism and the Freudian notion of the superego. The basic paradox of the superego also concerns a certain structural imbalance: the more we obey its command, the more we feel guilty, so that renunciation entails only a demand for more renunciation repentance more guilt — as in capitalism, where an increase in production to fill out the lack only widens the lack.[44]

Just as capital serves as its own internal, though openly productive limit, so too, as we have seen, desire serves as its own internal, though openly productive, limit. This is why postmodern theorists' celebration of new and fluid identities, etc., unwittingly reflect — even serve — the new strategies of power. But this is also why many of today's theorists' reliance on the rational autonomous ego completely misrepresents contemporary subjectivity and is tempted to treat a whole series of social upheavals from sexist and racist outbursts to the rise of fundamentalisms not as symptoms of this subjectivity, but as irrational remainders of the past which we still need to bring under rational control. As Žižek points out, however, in a society of universalized reflexivity and greater freedoms of choice, in a situation wherein 'the big Other *qua* the substance of our social being disintegrates, the unity of practice and its inherent reflection disintegrates into raw violence and its impotent, inefficient interpretation (. . .), the paradoxical [result is the] re-emergence of the brute Real of 'irrational' violence, impermeable and insensitive to reflexive interpretation'.[45]

Žižek's recourse to Lacanian psychoanalysis is meant to show how this series of upheavals, far from being a separate issue distinct from the operation of the political economy, is in fact its necessary obverse, its symptom. It is the contemporary subject, as an empty subject of desire that renders them structurally *necessary* events. Just as Freud was able to gather together a whole series of separate features (slips of the tongue, jokes, dreams, conversion symptoms, etc.) by linking them to the logic of the unconscious, so too Žižek gathers together a whole series of social symptoms as structurally dependent upon the logic of desire that *is* the capitalist motor.[46]

In order to grasp how Žižek links together this series of social symptoms, it is worth recalling our account of the Lacanian subject as a subject of desire. There, we saw that the two central elements that sustained our trust in the symbolic order (the big Other) was the *extraction* of a positive object, accompanied by symbolic prohibitions.

The capitalist erosion of the big Other's efficiency, therefore, throws the subject of desire into a panic. When symbolic authority *qua* prohibition gives way to a more permissive society, when objects of desire are more readily available and less subject to social prohibition (you are free to invent your own marital and/or sexual arrangements, however perverse these might appear; others will tolerate your actions and opinions), the social subject comes that much closer to realizing its desire. But, as our account of desire made clear, I hope, this proximity to fulfilment simply arouses anxiety. Why? Because it threatens to extinguish the subject as a subject of desire: a subject of desire sustains itself only on condition that its ultimate object of desire remains inaccessible. Thus, the structural consequence of the growing collapse of symbolic efficiency is not a healthy burgeoning of pleasurable experiences and increased well-being. Instead, it is a desperate attempt to cling to this kind of subjectivity by *making* the big Other exist. And in a situation of generalized cynicism, in the absence of symbolic faith, we witness 'the proliferation of different versions of *a big Other that actually exists, in the Real*, not merely as a symbolic fiction'.[47]

This is precisely the role that ethical committees, sex guides, and manuals of political correctness play;[48] or the role that various moral, political, and religious fundamentalisms play. They do not so much succeed in establishing some unitary empty prohibition characteristic of past subjectivities. Instead they are characterized more by a proliferation of rules and regulations that provide a whole host of imaginary ideals (about what to say, about what to eat, etc.). In the absence of symbolic faith, we attempt to recoup certainty with even greater urgency by means of the decentred sprouting of bureaucratic apparatuses.

This is one way to understand Hardt and Negri's claim that '[t]he anti-modern thrust that defines fundamentalisms might be better understood. . . not as a premodern but as a postmodern project'.[49] In a style reminiscent of Hobsbawm and Ranger's edited volume *The Invention of Tradition*,[50] they note that '[t]he "return to the traditional family" of the Christian fundamentalists is not backward-looking at all, but rather a new invention that is part of a political project against the contemporary social order'.[51] Similarly, Karen Armstrong, in her study of religious fundamentalisms, *The Battle for God*, strongly contests the widespread feeling that they are 'inherently conservative and wedded to the past,' instead portraying their ideas as 'essentially modern and highly innovative'.[52] According to Armstrong it is clear that fundamentalism 'is an essentially twentieth-century movement'.[53]

More direct, of course, is Žižek's claim that the rise of fundamentalisms is the inherent reverse of Capital's hegemonic sway. *'The more the logic of Capital becomes universal, the more its opposite will assume features of 'irrational fundamentalism'.* In other words, there is no way out as long as the universal dimension of our social formation remains defined in terms of Capital'.[54]

What unites these otherwise disparate phenomena is our contemporary subjective stance. The disintegration of our faith in the big Other, then, creates anxiety in subjects of desire and it becomes imperative that new obstacles arc introduced to regain a sense of balance. In other words, the logic of desire reproduces exactly the logic of capital which requires for its survival new frontiers, new enemies.

So when the symbolic Other does not succeed in meeting our expectations, we wax cynical and invent 'real' reasons for its failure. This logic, in other words, parallels the logic of fantasy I outlined earlier. In the absence of symbolic efficiency, what comes to the forefront is the real *cause* of desire (as distinct from the *object* of desire). What now appears centre stage is the (void-)cause of our desire which is misperceived as an obstacle: the soft permissive liberal, the Jew, the immigrant, the paedophile, the animal rights terrorist, etc.

This generates a whole matrix of modes of 'making the Other exist'. The Other can be made to exist by returning to basic traditional mores (as in various fundamentalisms), by complaining to the Other (as in our contemporary complaint culture),[55] by provoking the Other by cutting into the real of the body (as in body piercing, self-inflicted harm, suicide, various sadomasochistic practices in the visual arts, etc.),[56] by accusing the Other for allowing others to steal our way of life (as in various right wing discourses targeting immigrants, gypsy-travelers, etc.), by means of bypassing the Other through a direct reference to the real of science (as in the various attempts by committees to ground decisions upon an exhaustive calculus of risk based on their expert knowledge of the latest scientific technology), by positing an Other of the Other (as in various conspiracy theories).

Let us focus only on this last mode of making the Other exist. Since we can no longer sustain the efficiency of the Other through symbolic faith, we can only do so by reference to a *real* Other that accounts for the symbolic Other's inefficiency. In other words, '[t]he distrust of the big Other (the order of symbolic fictions), the subject's refusal to "take it seriously", relies on the belief that there is an "Other of the Other", that a secret, invisible and all-powerful agent actually pulls the strings and runs the show: behind the visible, public Power there is another obscene, invisible power structure'.[57] This, at least, would account for the recent popularity of movies and TV series that rely on conspiracy narratives.

In effect, Žižek argues that political, cinematic, and televisual conspiratorial narratives offer insights into the nature of contemporary conceptions of subjectivity and power relations. The study of conspiracies — all the way from J.F.K and Martin Luther King to *Arlington Road, Enemy of the State*, and *X-Men*, to *X Files* — is not normally taken seriously by mainstream academia, often finding refuge in the more marginal cultural studies departments. Conspiracy theories are viewed principally as odd curiosities that are interesting to survey but which, ultimately, are treated as irrational remainders that sit uneasily with, and which will soon be overcome by, increasingly rationalized and efficient corporate and state apparatuses. In direct contrast to this, Žižek invests such cultural phenomena with a dignity that places them at the heart of any serious engagement with political theory and philosophy.

Yet, insofar as the paranoid logic of conspiracies[58] betrays a last ditch effort to make the official social ordering of our polity (the symbolic Other) consistent, they can be seen as just one instantiation of the psychoanalytic category of fantasy. And if we take this observation seriously, it immediately becomes evident that fantasmatic narratives expressed at the margins of official public discourse can take on a content which need not be restricted to conspiratorial paranoia. Movies such as *The Truman Show, eXistenZ*, and *The Matrix*, or apocalyptic narratives — whether or not of a millenarian spirit — all become relevant exemplifications of this fantasmatic logic. In this view, fantasy provides a rationale that permits us to avoid confronting the Other's inconsistency and incompleteness, thereby generating an Other of the Other, a *real* Other of the symbolic Other. It is a rationale to which contemporary conditions readily lend themselves (including the increasingly disproportionate power invested in private individuals, and new technologies and popular shows such as the internet, GPSs, CCTVs, genetic technology, so-called 'reality TV' programmes like *Big Brother* and confessional-style talk shows, etc.).

But even if we accept Žižek's invocation of the Lacanian logic of desire to clarify the nature of capitalism and the symptoms of a decline in symbolic faith,[59] what alternative ways of thinking of emancipation does psychoanalytic theory make possible?[60] The first step in this process involves a more precise specification of the social fantasies that sustain the empty subject of capitalism.

Fantasies of Capitalism

How precisely does Žižek propose to analyze the discourse of capitalism in terms of the logic of desire and fantasy? If we return to capitalism's *de facto* privileging of contingency and partial fixation of meanings and identities, we must suppose with Žižek that this occurs within the context of a higher unacknowledged necessity. In psychoanalytic terms, the empty form of the logic of desire acquires its consistency only within the context of an overarching fantasmatic frame which must be made explicit. What then, does Žižek suppose, are capitalism's fantasies?

One way to approach this issue is to ask what *sustains* the social subject as empty. That is to say, how does the subject sustain the experience of his or her identity as *contingently* constituted? Žižek's central thesis is that this is possible on account of a disavowed social fantasy: we can accept contingency only on condition that a necessary 'illusion' remain protected. In this view, the contingency celebrated by capitalism is a false contingency because it is premised upon an unacknowledged underlying necessity. Contingency is bearable only because it is sustained by the potential for full control, the reassertion with even greater urgency of the subject as a fully conscious and rational ego able to master the ever-expanding realm of new choices opened up by the dissolution of sedimented social relations of traditional and modern society. In other words, we can accept contingency only because we secretly believe that this will ultimately provide us with the chance to literally become our own Gods. The widespread affirmation of freedom of choice and our belief in the American dream are simply publicly acceptable versions of the beatific aspect of this fantasy.

Equally important, however, is the inherently negative aspect of fantasy. If the beatific dimension of the social fantasy is best characterized by the potential for full control, the horrific dimension is, of course, the prospect of complete *lack* of control, of becoming a helpless victim. This, perhaps, is why Žižek claims that our repulsive fascination vis-á-vis the victim, of the human being as 'something that can be hurt' fits perfectly the logic of capitalism (all the way from the child as victim, the perceived proliferation of threats to our health and security, the uncomfortable feeling evoked by the sight of street dwellers, the strange attraction exerted by disaster scenes, sentimental humanitarianism in the face of horrific war tales of rape and torture, to the whole Western culture of complaint).[61] Indirect proof of this comes from our ambivalent response to the victim. The victim arouses the twin feelings of superiority (which leads to a desire to maintain the position of victimhood through, for example, charity or humanitarian aid) and anxiety-disgust (since more and more we can see ourselves as potential victims and we would rather not be reminded of it). This means that under the right conditions, the victim can come to be seen as that part of ourselves which we would like to keep out of sight or eliminate rather than confront (by dispersing immigrants throughout our country, by rounding up and isolating the homeless and other social 'rejects'). The exact obverse to this, though, is that as soon as the victim decides to become politically active, as soon as he or she decides to take direct action; in short as soon as she or he 'no longer behaves like a victim, but wants to strike back on its own, it magically turns all of a sudden into a terrorist/fundamentalist/drug-trafficking Other'.[62]

Of course, this account of capitalism's fantasies (framed in terms of full control or lack of control) is a kind of 'archetype'. That is to say, its specific incarnations will be coloured by the concrete context within which the logic of capital manages to install itself. But the central insight that psychoanalysis brings to bear on this type of analysis is its highlighting not of the actual concrete content of fantasy but rather of its function. In this view, the role of fantasy is not so much to provide an alternative discourse with which to make sense of our world (or, more precisely, to make sense of the big Other's failures), but rather to provide us with a way of organizing our enjoyment, our *jouissance*, our mode of being. As I have already pointed out, this mode of enjoyment is sustained by a reference to an obstacle *qua* cause of desire (as opposed to an object of desire). Just as with the logic of capital, so too the logic of desire is able to sustain itself on the basis of a (constitutive) outside, typically embodied by a threat posed to our most precious possessions (our way of life, our children, etc.), and evoked by an enemy that must be extinguished (the Jew, the immigrant, the hooligan, the dangerous criminal, the paedophile, the fundamentalist, etc.).

This has crucial implications for ideological analysis and critique. It means, for example, that what is responsible for Power's grip is not so much the false narrative that fantasy offers us but the mode of enjoyment it makes possible. This is precisely why the critique of ideology cannot proceed on the basis of rational argumentation or on the basis of pointing out how the fantasmatic narrative does not correspond to the 'facts of the matter'. The fantasmatic scenario provides us with the elements of our very being, it sustains us as subjects of desire, and has little to do with some sort of reality 'out there'. In short, its function is to cover up the lack in the big Other, the inner antagonism of the symbolic order itself.

This is also why it is insufficient to object to this analysis with the question, 'But what if our children really *are* victims? What if these religious groups really *are* fundamentalist terrorists? What if Jews and immigrants really *are* stealing our jobs and raping our women?' The point is that the central ideological ingredient is to be located in the *mode* of enjoyment which is indifferent to so-called 'facts of the matter'. This is the reason Žižek emphasizes that

[w]hat sets in motion this logic of the 'theft of enjoyment' is ... not immediate social reality — the reality [for example] of different ethnic communities living closely together — but the *inner antagonism inherent in these communities*. It is possible to have a multitude of ethnic communities living side by side without racial tensions (like the Amish and neighbouring communities in Pennsylvania); on the other hand, one does not need a lot of 'real' Jews to impute to them some mysterious enjoyment that threatens us (it is a well-known fact that in Nazi Germany, anti-Semitism was most ferocious in those parts where there were almost no Jews; in today's ex-East Germany, the anti-Semitic Skinheads outnumber Jews by ten to one). Our perception of 'real' Jews is always mediated by a symbolic-ideological structure which tries to cope with social antagonism: the real 'secret' of the Jew is our own antagonism.[63]

So where does this leave us? Does this mean that we should allow terrorists, paedophiles, etc., free rein even if we all agree that they *are* a threat to our security and well-being? How, in other words should we deal with such pressing issues? In order to avoid a potentially fatal misunderstanding, it is crucial to point out here that when, for example, Žižek suggests that '[t]he way to break out of this vicious [fantasmatic] circle is not to fight the "irrational" nationalist particularism[s] but to invent forms of political practice that contain a dimension of universality beyond Capital,'[64] his central target is the *enjoyment* structured by capitalist fantasies. According to him, the ultimate political or critical–ideological aim should be to 'search for ways to sap the force of this underlying fantasy frame itself—in short, to perform something akin to the Lacanian "going through the fantasy" '.[65] This does not mean that it is possible to avoid dealing with pressing threats to our security and well being. At this level we definitely *do* need to be pragmatic, and appeals to mainstream political science and normative political theory would not at all go amiss here. His point, however, is that such pragmatic and rational approaches typically intervene at a superficial symptomal level that leaves the fantasmatic object-cause of desire intact. In this view, effective critical interventions must be made with an eye to traversing the social fantasy, not simply in reference to commonly accepted political discourses that leave it undisturbed.

Modes of Subjectivity, the Depoliticized Economy, and Authentic Acts

If we accept Žižek's claim that today's socio-political symptoms are a direct result of the kind of subjectivity that the logic of capitalism promotes; if we accept that they are a structural consequence of the particular stance the subject of desire adopts toward the big Other and the fantasies that underlie it; this suggests that the 'way out' must involve the exhortation to a new type of ethical stance (an ethics of the drive) and a correspondingly appropriate subjectivity (the subject of the drive). But if a return to traditionalism is out of the question (since any such return will in any case always be mediated by the modern cut[66]), if we accept that today's big Other of capitalist hegemony is defunct (due to the structural symptoms it gives rise to in the face of its inconsistencies), and if we follow Žižek in supposing communism to be an inherently capitalist fantasy,[67] how can we think of plausible ways out?

Though Žižek concedes that it may not be possible to undermine the global capitalist system, 'at least not in the foreseeable future,'[68] he implies that it is nonetheless crucial to acknowledge that the current capitalist hegemony promotes a certain kind of subject (the subject of desire) which is misperceived by most theorists as a liberated conscious ego. His central thesis, therefore, suggests that the continued depoliticization of the economy sustains precisely this misperceived (decentred, non-autonomous) subject of desire which is fully responsible for the proliferation of paranoid fantasies of the 'Other of the Other' sort and the emergence of populist New Right movements which are today 'the main obstacle to the realization of the very (feminist, ecological . . .) demands on which postmodern forms of political subjectivity focus'.[69]

What makes Žižek's calls for a radical repoliticization of the economy[70] (as distinct from half-hearted neo-liberal compromises) appear impossible, as implausible demands, is not, of course, their impracticality (as if the facade of economic expertise was able to conceal their retrodictive rationalizations of decisions already taken by private supranational corporations). Rather, what sustains this exclusionary official public discourse are the social subject's disavowed social fantasies and their constitutive 'threats' — those, in other words, who take advantage of our present system, like single mothers, immigrants, prisoners, etc. It is precisely there that the battle against capitalism should properly be fought (as opposed to engaging only in rational-deliberative political argument which is *sustained* by these social fantasies). A properly authentic, ethical act, therefore, is one that manages to effect a kind of 'crossing of the social fantasy,'[71] thereby exposing the lack in the big Other, the ultimate impotence of the dominant politico-economic discourse.[72]

In sum, then, what is most traumatic is not that I am subject to the rule of the big Other, to the Master. All our complaints and appeals to justice conceal their true function, namely to *maintain* the big Other and the *jouissance* it makes possible for us. Far more traumatic is the possibility that the big Other does not exist. *This* is ultimately what we cannot accept as subjects of desire and this is ultimately the reason for our ready recourse to fantasies of the 'Other of the Other' who 'steal' our enjoyment. This is why, for Žižek, the aim of ideological critique is to create the conditions in which we can 'experience how there is nothing "behind" it, and how fantasy masks precisely this "nothing"'.[73] And, of course, this 'crossing of the fantasy' ushers in a distinctively novel ethical horizon and a corresponding mode of subjectivity.

Strategic Perspectives on 'Traversing the Fantasy'

Given this fantasmatic approach to ideological analysis, what kinds of strategies does it open up for ideological critique? How might we think the notion of 'crossing the social fantasy' in more concrete terms? I will discuss two suggestions Žižek offers.

First, we might try to *deflate* the publicly supported imaginary ideals, our precious treasures, that appear to be threatened by the intrusion of an evil menace. Let us take the Jew as an example of one such perceived threat. Žižek claims that Freud attempted just such a strategic move by portraying the Jew as someone who does not in fact possess the precious treasure that anti-Semites insist on imputing to him:

> What Freud did [in his *Moses and Monotheism*] was ... the exact opposite of Arnold Schoenberg, for example, who scornfully dismissed Nazi racism as a pale imitation of the self-comprehension of the Jews as the elected people: by way of an almost masochistic inversion, Freud targeted Jews themselves and endeavored to prove that their founding father, Moses, was Egyptian. Notwithstanding the historic (in)accuracy of this thesis, what really matters is its discursive strategy: to demonstrate that Jews are already in themselves 'decentred,' that their 'originality' is a bricolage. The difficulty does not reside in Jews but in the transference of the anti-Semite who thinks that Jews 'really possess it,' *agalma*, the secret of their power: the anti-Semite is the one who 'believes in the Jew,' so the only way effectively to undermine anti-Semitism is to contend that *Jews do not possess 'it'*.[74]

We immediately see how, in the absence of the fantasmatic analysis supporting this approach, this strategy appears counterintuitive in achieving its aims. Without its proper theoretical contextualization, in other words, this strategy would itself no doubt be construed as counterproductive at best and anti-Semitic at worst. In a homologous way, we could think of a similarly unsettling strategy that targets the special way paedophiles regard children. The equivalent strategy here would, of course, not be the 'spontaneous' one of demonizing paedophiles and emphasizing the innocence of our children; just as Freud did not demonize the anti-Semite or elevate the special traits of Jewish culture. These approaches would simply exacerbate the problem by heightening the privileged status of the victim, making their torture and rape all that harder to resist. Instead, the equivalent strategy would be to emphasize how children are in fact not as innocent as we might imagine them, to highlight their already polymorphously perverse sexuality, etc.[75]

If the first strategy involves devaluing the object of desire we think the Other has stolen (or threatens to steal) from us, a second possible strategy might involve *confronting* the social subject with the obstacle *qua cause* of desire. This obstacle is often perceived in terms of a threat, as is the case in UFO conspiracy theories, for example. According to one such typical account, the powers that be conceal all official 'top secret' information on alien sightings, space ships, experiments on aliens, and deny all knowledge of such things, including any cabalic 'deals' or 'concessions' they have made with them. Žižek's point here, however, is that the

> ultimate ground of the fear of 'aliens' is that they are usually conceived of as a force against which there is no possible defence; here, however, one has to be more precise: those who are helpless against the 'aliens' are not us but those in power. An encounter with 'aliens' would lay open the ultimate imposture of the Master, it would sap our (unconscious) belief in the Power's omnipotence. This experience of how 'the throne is empty' (of how the big Other does not exist) is bound to trigger panic ... [But] the ultimate root of our fear of 'aliens' is not their physical menace as such but their ultimate motives and intentions, which remain completely impenetrable and unknown to us,[76]

thereby embodying perfectly (though in inverted form) the lack in the big Other. In short, the (fantasmatic) 'threat' of aliens, far from undermining the hegemonic sway of the big Other only serves to bolster it.

It is in this context that Žižek's claim that a certain kind of *ecological* movement holds the most promise for helping us 'invent forms of political practice that contain a dimension of universality beyond Capital. 'Why? As he puts it,

> [t]he crucial, hitherto underestimated ideological impact of the coming ecological crisis will be precisely to make the 'collapse of the big Other' part of our everyday experience, i.e., to sap this unconscious belief in the 'big Other' of power: already the Chernobyl catastrophe made ridiculously obsolete such notions as 'national sovereignty,' exposing the power's ultimate impotence. Our 'spontaneous' ideological reaction to it, of course, is to have recourse to the fake premodern forms of reliance on the 'big Other' ('New Age consciousness'; the balanced circuit of Nature, etc.). Perhaps, however, our very physical survival hinges on our ability to consummate the act of assuming fully the 'nonexistence of the Other,' [of abandoning our attempts to find another Other behind the big Other].[77]

Conclusion

Even if we accept this essay's reconstruction of Žižek's account of the relation between Lacanian psychoanalysis and capitalism, we are still left with at least two important and pressing questions. First, what kind of ethical horizon does Žižek's critique of capitalist ideology present us with? And second, what research questions does it raise? It is around these questions that I will organize my concluding remarks.

The name Žižek gives to the ethical horizon opened up by his Lacanian Marxism is the 'ethics of the drive' or, alternatively, the 'ethics of the real'. In Lacanian terms, it is an ethics that is opposed not only to an imaginary ethics of the Good, but also to an ethics of desire which privileges the contingent link between the empty place of power and the various imaginary goods that seek to hegemonize it. Though Žižek agrees that capitalist ideology presents itself as the necessary placeholder of the empty space of power, he argues that the resistance to the visibility of its contingent hegemony resides in a series of underlying fantasies, and not simply in the exclusionary public discourse they support. In addition, however, it relies upon a particular ethical stance which corresponds to a precisely defined subjectivity, namely, the subject of desire. To an ethics of desire Žižek opposes an ethics of the drive.

What separates desire from drive is, as we have seen, fantasy. And thus the basic formula that summarizes the passage from one type of ethical stance to the other is cast in terms of 'crossing the fantasy'. But what exactly lies on the other side of fantasy? Can we make more precise the horizon of an ethics of the drive?

It seems that Žižek cannot but respond negatively to this question, and for good reason. We can appreciate why this must be so if we recall that his argument relies on a Kojevian view of history as applied to the field of subjectivity. More specifically, he implies that such a history is punctuated by cuts, each of which signal a mutation in human subjectivity. Though such a historical thesis awaits a more systematic elaboration, we can perhaps hazard one possible formulation of the supporting conjectures underpinning such a thesis: the passage from premodern subjectivity to modern subjectivity (and the accompanying shifts in socio-political arrangements) was made possible by the emergence of monotheistic religions; while the passage from modern to postmodern subjectivity (and the accompanying shifts in socio-political arrangements) was made possible by the scientific revolution and the birth of capitalism.[78] In this view, monotheistic Prohibition marks the primordial repression that gives birth to a whole series of fantasies that support socio-political discourse; and the subsequent modern and postmodern eras presuppose a subjectivity that operates *within* this fantasmatic framework. Žižek's anti-capitalism, then, amounts to nothing short of a call to another fundamental mutation in human subjectivity corresponding to the passage through fantasy and entailing an ethical stance that is adequate to this task.

The prospect of a fundamental mutation, however, evokes horror. Just as the demand to replace polytheism with monotheism, or secularism with monotheism could not but be perceived as idealist, even terroristic, so too will the anti-capitalist demand to move beyond fantasy. Why? Because it implies a complete revamping of our economic, social, and political institutional arrangements, and the standards of evaluation they presuppose. This, ultimately, is why it is not possible to give concrete content to the new ethics of the drive. What will emerge on the other side of fantasy cannot be predicted in advance, much less judged on the basis of contemporary standards of evaluation. Any such attempt to predict outcomes can only rely on current standards and ideals, reducing reformist cautionary projects to a consequentialist calculus that seeks foundational guarantees rooted in our current ethico-political horizon. It would simply reiterate through other means the thesis that there is an 'Other of the Other'.

This, indeed, gives some rationale to Žižek's 'returns' to the Stalinist terror, the Nazi horror, or the various ethnic wars.[79] When he subjects these phenomena to analytical treatment, his aim is not directly to propose a new concrete socio-political framework which would prevent such atrocities in the future. He does not argue that we need more human rights, more political will, more sophisticated legal systems, etc. Instead, his aim is to show that what is responsible for such 'extraordinary' outbursts is nothing other than the very 'ordinary' and normal contemporary subject, with all his or her foibles (i.e., the subject of desire) and that we *must* find a way out, a way *through* fantasy, a way to fully assume that 'there is no Other of the Other' and thus no longer be 'bothered' by the lack in the Other. Žižek effectively implies that the modality of such outbursts is simply unavailable under the regime of an ethics of the drive; that the kind of subjectivity which makes them possible is absent. Thus, his aim is a purely negative one: he cannot offer up a concrete vision of what such a regime would look like, only what it would *not* look like. In this view, our passage through the fundamental fantasy of capitalism will await the spontaneous invention of new models of socio-political arrangement, just as the spontaneous formation of the Paris commune can be seen as a model for Marx's communism. This is, perhaps, one way to read Žižek's call to the 'socialization of productive forces'. This empty signifier is one that has been foreclosed by current capitalist discourse. His recourse to it, therefore, invests it with a dimension of impossibility, a radical emptiness that new forms of post-capitalist socio-economic arrangements will attempt to fill with concrete meaning.

And yet, even if we accept his implicit argument that negative reasons (to overcome social symptoms, to acquire a new relation to our suffering) are sufficient to prompt us to move ahead, to explore a new ethical horizon; even if we accept that he cannot offer up concrete visions of what this new regime would look like in toto; we are still tempted to advance a whole series of research questions this line of inquiry throws up. I will propose two sets of questions, ranging from the more abstract to the more detailed.

One such set begins by asking for a more precise specification of the historical thesis I referred to earlier, including a more systematic argument demonstrating the supposedly monolithic nature of the capitalist logic — for it is this singular logic (as opposed to a plurality of capitalist logics) that renders its structural affinity with the logic of desire plausible. In addition, however, we should also insist on a more precise specification of what in contemporary political theory, political science, and political practice, we can legitimately engage with. In other words, can we engage in contemporary empirical and normative debates productively, or must we — as may be implied by his sometimes dismissive language — resign ourselves to a stark all or nothing choice? Should we always treat appeals to interdisciplinary 'compromise' or 'consensus' as evils to be avoided at all costs? In other words, if we were to revisit specific, delimited (non-Lacanian) domains of political research with the aim of revamping outdated ontological and epistemological assumptions, what elements and what results could we productively rearticulate to a Lacanian approach to political theory?

A second set of research questions probes the link between Lacanian categories developed within a clinical context and Lacanian categories deployed for purposes of socio-political analysis. One such question concerns the relation between fantasies (in the plural) on the one hand, and the fundamental fantasy (in the singular) on the other. In Žižek's account, it appears that the content of social fant*asies* (in the plural) is subject to repeated displacement, just as our publicly-articulated discourses are subject to displacements and condensations. In this view, fantasies are formal structures whose variables can take on a wide variety of substitutable contents. The cause of desire *qua* obstacle, for example, can appear as the Jew, the alien, the paedophile, the immigrant, etc. Proceeding by analogy with the clinic, therefore, it is supposed that this series of displacements/substitutions is governed by an underlying rule given by the *fundamental* fantasy. At the social level, of course, Žižek claims that this is nothing other than the 'depoliticization of the economy'. What is not clear, however, is precisely what the difference is between crossing any one of a whole array of social fantasies (in the plural) and crossing the fundamental social fantasy (in the singular). Here, I think, it is too easy to abstain from offering any response, even if we accept the necessarily negative gesture that this ethical move entails.

Finally, though Žižek *does* give examples of subjects who act ethically (i.e., in accordance with the dictates of the drive) from *within* the horizon of fantasy,[80] there is next to nothing concerning the *subject of the drive* (i.e., the subject who emerges on the 'other' side of fantasy), and — most urgently — the implications this carries for the very possibility of community.

In order to bring this last issue better into focus, let us for a moment recall Žižek's implied historical thesis, where it was suggested that crossing the fundamental fantasy would involve, in some sense, leaving behind the whole fantasy structure installed by the Prohibition of monotheistic religions. What is required, here, is not so much an account of what will follow in concrete and predictive detail, but a precise, even if speculative, *theoretical* account of what the possible modalities of a subject of the drive might be at the *social* level. In other words, what kind of *community* is (even theoretically) possible for subjects of the drive? What insights can Lacanian clinical theory offer us? Since a Lacanian conception of community eschews ideas of shared values or common symbolic identifications; and since it suggests that our social bond should also not be based on a common fantasmatic transgression (which makes possible a community of subjects of desire), what other ways are there of thinking a community of subjects? Indeed, is a *social* subject of the drive possible?

JASON GLYNOS
University of Essex

NOTES

1 Slavoj Žižek, *The Metastases of Enjoyment* (London, Verso, 1994), p. ii. For useful critical comments on a draft version of this paper I thank Yannis Stavrakakis. For detailed and helpful editorial comments — not to mention patience — I thank Edmond Wright.

2 Several scholars have elaborated in detail the notion of the Lacanian subject. Within a clinical context, for example, Bruce Fink has fleshed this out in terms of a three-fold distinction between the subject of demand, the subject of desire, and the subject of drive: see Bruce Fink, *A Clinical Introduction to Lacanian Psychoanalysis: Theory and Technique* (Cambridge, Harvard University Press, 1997). Within philosophical ethics, Alenka Zupancic has linked these subjective stances with the corresponding philosophical ethics of the communitarian Good, Kant's purity of the moral law, and the psychoanalytic drive: see Alenka Zupancic, *Ethics of the Real* (London, Verso, 2000). Renata Salecl, for her part, has periodized each of these ethical modalities of the subject as a function of their relative predominance in any one historical epoch. Thus, for example, premodern subjectivity is seen as governed primarily by the demands made by an overarching common Good, whether in terms of an Aristotelian ethics of moderation or in terms of a utilitarian calculus of pleasures and pains. Likewise, postmodern subjectivity is construed as an intensification of the modern subject's paradoxical attempt to both avoid and cling to its objects of desire: see Renata Salecl, *(Per)Versions of Love and Hate* (London, Verso, 1998).

3 Karl Marx and Friedrich Engels, 'Manifesto of the Communist Party' in Robert C. Tucker, ed., *The Marx-Engels Reader* (New York, W.W. Norton, 1972), p. 475.

4 ibid., p. 476.

5 ibid., p. 476.

6 Slavoj Žižek, *Tarrying with the Negative* (Durham, Duke University Press, 1993), p. 209.

7 Slavoj Žižek, *The Ticklish Subject* (London, Verso, 1999), pp. 358.

8 Review posted at barnesandnoble.com/ (accessed 25 August 2000).

9 Judith Butler, Ernesto Laclau, and Slavoj Žižek, *Contingency, Hegemony, Universality* (London, Verso, 2000), p. 329, note 11.

10 Michael Hardt, and Antonio Negri, *Empire* (Cambridge, Harvard University Press, 2000)

11 Marx, from Hardt and Negri, p. 222.

12 ibid., p. 222.

13 ibid., p. 224.

14 ibid., p. 227.

15 ibid., p. 227.

16 On this point, see, for example, George Ritzer, 'Obscene from any Angle: Fast Food, Credit Cards, Casinos and Consumers,' *Third Text* 51 (2000), p. 17.

17 Hardt and Negri, p. 227.

18 Slavoj Žižek, *The Ticklish Subject* (London, Verso, 1999), p. 356.

19 Ernesto Laclau, *New Reflections on the Revolution of Our Time* (London, Verso, 1990), p. 45.

20 See, for example, Mark E. Warren, ed., *Democracy and Trust* (Cambridge, CUP, 1999); John Dunn, 'Trust' in his *The History of Political Theory and Other Essays* (Cambridge: CUP, 1996); Barbara Misztal, Trust in Modern Societies (Cambridge, Polity Press, 1996). Related texts include Jeffrey Goldfarb, *The Cynical Society: the Culture of Politics and the Politics of Culture in American Life* (Chicago: Univ. of Chicago Press, 1991); Richard Stivers, *The Culture of Cynicism: American Morality in Decline* (Oxford: Blackwell, 1994); Michael Lerner, *The Politics of Meaning: Restoring Hope and Possibility in an Age of Cynicism* (Reading, Mass: Addison-Wesley, 1996).

21 Slavoj Žižek, *The Ticklish Subject* (London, Verso, 1999), p. 319. As he puts it, 'Descartes' 'voluntarism' (see his infamous statement that $2 + 2$ would be 5 if such were God's Will . . .) is the necessary obverse of modern scientific knowledge'.

22 Slavoj Žižek, *The Ticklish Subject* (London, Verso, 1999), pp. 319–20.

23 ibid., pp. 332.

24 ibid., pp. 334.

25 ibid., pp. 336–7.

26 ibid., pp. 337. 'The freedom of decision enjoyed by the subject of the 'risk society' is not the freedom of someone who can freely choose his destiny, but the anxiety-provoking freedom of someone who is constantly compelled to make decisions without being aware of their consequences,' pp. 338.

27 ibid., pp. 360.

28 ibid., pp. 342.

29 ibid., pp. 342.

30 Richard Sennett, *The Corrosion of Character* (New York, W.W. Norton, 1998), p. 99.

31 Slavoj Žižek, *Tarrying with the Negative* (Durham, Duke University Press, 1993), p. 216.

32 Hardt and Negri, p. 138. Of course, highlighting this parallel between the discourses of anti-essentialism and corporate capital is not meant to belittle the valuable theoretical work underpinning the former. On the contrary, a Lacanian perspective puts the lie to such simplistic parallels by emphasizing that what is significant in the foregrounding of fluidity, uncertainty, and undecidability, is not the value they somehow inherently embody but rather the *stance* subjects adopt toward them. It suggests we investigate what array of subjective *relations* to uncertainty and undecidability are possible. How, for example, might we account for the reluctance of workers to question this call to the ideal of contingency? Or how might we think the possibility that such a call might *reinforce* the kind of subjectivity characterised by an ethics of desire? This already hints at the significance for Žižek of the category of fantasy which will be discussed shortly.

33 On this, see also Zygmunt Bauman, 'Scene and Obscene: Another Hotly Contested Opposition,' *Third Text* 51 (2000), p. 5; and Richard Sennett,

The Corrosion of Character (New York, W.W. Norton, 1998), especially pp. 114–116.

34 On this see also, Žižek, *The Ticklish Subject*, pp. 350–358, 395–7.

35 Hardt and Negri p. 234.

36 Hardt and Negri p. 235.

37 Slavoj Žižek, 'Everything Provokes Fascism,' *Assemblage* 33 (1997), p. 61.

38 Slavoj Žižek, *The Fragile Absolute* (London, Verso, 2000), pp. 23–4.

39 For a similar remark on the link between Marxism and psychoanalysis, see Ernesto Laclau, 'Psychoanalysis and Marxism' in his *New Reflections on the Revolution of Our Time* (London, Verso, 1990), p. 96: 'This indicates the direction and the way in which a possible confluence of (post-) Marxism and psychoanalysis is conceivable, neither as the addition of a supplement to the former by the latter nor as the introduction of a new causal element—the unconscious instead of the economy—but as the coincidence of the two, around the logic of the signifier as a logic of unevenness and dislocation, a coincidence grounded on the fact that the latter is the logic which presides over the possibility/impossibility of the constitution of *any* identity'.

40 On the notion of 'false acts,' see Slavoj Žižek, 'Class Struggle or Postmodernism? No Thanks!' in Judith Butler et al., *Contingency, Hegemony, Universality* (London, Routledge, 2000), p. 126. For examples of 'authentic acts,' see Žižek, *ibid.*, p. 122.

41 Žižek, *The Ticklish Subject*, p. 341.

42 ibid., p. 355.

43 ibid., p. 355.

44 Žižek, *Tarrying with the Negative*, pp. 210–11. Here, perhaps, we could pose a research question based on the hypothesis that, insofar as the psychic structure predominant in women is shared by late capitalist discourse, the former would feel more at 'home' with the latter—at least more so than their male partners. Would this not offer a plausible explanation for the much touted crisis that men currently face?

45 Žižek, *The Ticklish Subject*, p. 346.

46 On the relation between contemporary advertising, capitalism, and the logic of desire, see Yannis Stavrakakis, 'On the Critique of Advertising Discourse: A Lacanian View,' *Third Text* 51 (2000), p. 85.

47 Žižek, *The Ticklish Subject*, p. 362.

48 Žižek, *Tarrying with the Negative*, pp. 213–4.

49 Hardt and Negri, p. 149.

50 Eric Hobsbawm and Terence Ranger, eds., *The Invention of Tradition* (Cambridge, Cambridge University Press, 1983).

51 Hardt and Negri, p. 148.

52 Karen Armstrong, *The Battle for God: Fundamentalism in Judaism, Christianity and Islam* (London, HarperCollins, 2000), p. x.

53 ibid., p. xi.

54 Žižek, *Tarrying with the Negative* p. 220.

55 The subject of complaint effectively accuses the Other of its inefficiency and blames it for what has supposedly been stolen from him or her (on account of past injustices, etc.). Thus, Žižek asks, '[i]s not the "culture of complaint" therefore today's version of hysteria, of the hysterical impossible demand addressed to the Other, a demand that actually wants to be rejected, since the subject grounds his/her existence in his/her complaint?' Žižek, *The Ticklish Subject*, p. 361.

56 See, for example, Žižek, *The Ticklish Subject*, pp. 372, 398. See also Renata Salecl, *(Per)Versions of Love and Hate* (London, Verso, 1998), Chapter 7.

57 Žižek, *The Ticklish Subject*, p. 362.

58 See also Jodi Dean, *Aliens in America: Conspiracy Cultures from Outerspace to Cyberspace* (Ithaca, Cornell University Press, 1998), Mark Fenster, *Conspiracy Theories: Secrecy and Power in American Culture* (Minneapolis, University of Minnesota Press, 1999), George Marcus, ed., *Paranoia within Reason: A Casebook on Conspiracy as Explanation* (Chicago, University of Chicago Press, 1999), Timothy Melly, *Empire of Conspiracy. The Culture of Paranoia in Postwar America* (Ithaca, Cornell University Press, 2000), Devon Jackson, *Conspiranoia* (New York, Plume, 2000), Patrick O'Donnell, *Latent Destinies: Cultural Paranoia and Contemporary US Narrative* (Durham, Duke University Press, 2000), and the huge number of internet sites devoted to conspiracy theories.

59 Žižek summarizes the structural effects of the fall of the symbolic Other: 'This disintegration of paternal authority has two facets. On the one hand, symbolic prohibitive norms are increasingly replaced by imaginary ideals (of social success, of bodily fitness ...); on the other, the lack of symbolic prohibition is supplemented by the re-emergence of ferocious superego figures. So we have a subject who is extremely narcissistic — who perceives everything as a potential threat to his precarious imaginary balance (take the universalization of the logic of victim; every contact with another human being is experienced as a potential threat: if the other person smokes, if he casts a covetous glance at me, he is already hurting me); far from allowing him to float freely in his undisturbed balance, however, this narcissistic self-enclosure leaves the subject to the (not so) tender mercies of the superego injunction to enjoy'. (Žižek, *The Ticklish Subject*, p. 368.)

60 Here is how Žižek poses the problematic: 'The task of today's thought is thus double: on the one hand, how to repeat the Marxist 'critique of political economy' without the utopian-ideological notion of Communism as its inherent standard; on the other, how to imagine actually breaking out of the capitalist horizon without falling into the trap of returning to the eminently premodern notion of a balanced, (self-)restrained society (the "pre-Cartesian" temptation which most of today's ecology succumbs)'. (Žižek, *The Fragile Absolute*, pp. 19–20.)

61 Žižek, *The Fragile Absolute*, p. 60.
62 ibid., p. 60.
63 Žižek, *Tarrying with the Negative*, p. 205.
64 ibid., p. 220.
65 ibid., p. 213.
66 Žižek, *The Fragile Absolute*, p. 33, 19–20.
67 ibid., p. 19.
68 Žižek, *The Ticklish Subject*, p. 352.
69 ibid., p. 356.
70 Here we must assume — for purposes of consistency — that Žižek's call to a 'return to the primacy of the economy' is different in kind from the types of return advocated by third way theorists, environmentalists, etc. Of central importance, perhaps, is not so much a return per se as it is the *way* this return is characterized.
71 As to the nature of this act, Žižek notes that 'the authentic act that I accomplish is always by definition a foreign body, an intruder which simultaneously attracts/fascinates and repels me, so that if and when I come too close to it, this leads to my *aphanisis*, self-erasure. If there is a subject to the act, it is not the subject of subjectivization, of integrating the act into the universe of symbolic integration and recognition, of assuming the act as "my own", but, rather, an uncanny "acephalous" subject through which the act takes place as that which is "in him more than himself"(. . .) — in the act, the subject, as Lacan puts it, *posits himself as his own cause*, and is no longer determined by the decentred object-cause. (. . .) — this act is precisely something which unexpectedly "just occurs", it is an occurrence which also (and even most) surprises its agent itself (after an authentic act, my reaction is always "Even I don't know how I was able to do that, it just happened!") (. . .) (. . .) The paradox of the act thus lies in the fact that although it is not 'intentional' in the usual sense of the term of consciously willing it, it is nevertheless accepted as something for which its agent is fully responsible — "I cannot do otherwise, yet I am none the less fully free in doing it" (. . .) (. . .) Within the horizon of what precedes the act, the act always and by definition appears as a change 'from Bad to Worse' (the usual criticism of conservatives against revolutionaries: yes, the situation is bad, but your solution is even worse). The proper heroism of the act is fully to assume this Worse. This means that there is none the less something inherently "terroristic" in every authentic act, in its gesture of thoroughly redefining the "rules of the game", inclusive of the very basic self-identity of its perpetrator — a proper political act unleashes the force of negativity that shatters the very foundations of our being [as a subject of desire]. . . . [T]he horrible experience of the Stalinist political terror should not lead us into abandoning the principle of terror itself — one should search even more stringently for the "good terror": Žižek, *The Ticklish Subject*, pp. 374–8.

See also pp. 391–2. For a contemporary example of someone making an authentic political act, see Žižek's analysis of the Mary Kay Letourneau case at pp. 381–8.

72 And here it is important to note that when Žižek talks of the 'inefficiency' or the 'collapse' of the big Other through today's universalized reflexivization of society, this does not necessarily translate into a change in the dominant terms of contemporary political debate. The big Other *does not* vanish. We simply relate to it in a different way. In this view, the intimations of the lack in the big Other have resulted not in an ethical confrontation with it, but rather in a desperate attempt to escape it by appealing to underlying social fantasies that fill it in. In other words, while it may be true that the typical subject is a cynical subject who comes to rely less on the symbolic order and more on the fantasies that support it, the crucial point is that the big Other itself remains intact, thereby continuing to regulate our public life without putting into question its injustices and inequalities. As Žižek puts it, '[w]hat I am running away from when I voluntarily take refuge in servitude is thus the traumatic confrontation with the big Other's ultimate impotence and imposture': Žižek, *Tarrying with the Negative* (Durham, Duke University Press, 1993), p. 235.

73 Slavoj Žižek, *The Sublime Object of Ideology* (London, Verso, 1989), p. 126.

74 Žižek, *Tarrying with the Negative*, pp. 220–1.

75 On this, see Dany Nobus's perspicacious analysis in his 'Arresting Innocence: On the Social Symptom of Child Abuse' (unpublished, 2000). Of course this strategy (regarding both the Jew and the Paedophile) does not mean that their offences should go unpunished. The point, however, is that without intervening with an eye on the fantasy structuring the social symptoms, not only do we miss an opportunity to sap the *jouissance* invested in them, we often in fact simply reinforce it.

76 Žižek, *Tarrying with the Negative*, pp. 235–6.

77 ibid., p. 237.

78 Perhaps we could say that, paralleling this historical account of subjectivity, is a corresponding account of responsibility, especially in relation to the notion of Evil. In this view, for premodern subjects, Evil was seen as 'out there' and thus external to them. Though, for example, Adam and Eve were responsible for succumbing to the temptations proffered by the Devil, the Devil himself was seen as separate and distinct from them, as having nothing to do with them. This can be contrasted with the typical modern subject, for whom Evil is invariably regarded as its own creation, and for which she/he is ultimately responsible (as in the Evil of Frankenstein's monster, of Hiroshima and Nagasaki, of environmental destruction, of computers causing havoc, etc.).

79 See, for example, Slavoj Žižek, *Plague of Fantasies* (London, Verso, 1997), pp. 54–64; Žižek 'Class Struggle or Postmodernism? No Thanks!,' pp. 124–6

(see note 40); and Žižek, *Tarrying with the Negative* (Durham, Duke University Press, 1993), Chapter 6.

80 Witness his frequent references to Antigone, Sygne de Coufontaine and Mary Kay Letourneau.

Absolute Freedom and Major Structural Change

Elizabeth Wright recognised that in terms of the reception of Lacan's work in English-speaking universities the contribution of Slavoj Žižek occupies a special place. This issue of *Paragraph*, which she and Edmond Wright conceived jointly, is an excellent opportunity to reflect upon Žižek's by now very considerable contribution. The importance of his work was obvious from the first of his books in English, *The Sublime Object of Ideology*.[1] One of the remarkable features of this remarkable work, as I see it, is the way it captures and conveys some of the sense of what made Lacan's work so exciting to a generation or two that had come under his influence in France from the early fifties through to the eighties. It captured the novelty of Lacan's thinking about language and the unconscious and, indeed, the radical nature of the unconscious itself; just as it conveyed the sense of what might otherwise look like empty rhetoric, namely that psychoanalysis is a radical and subversive doctrine whose practice calls into question dominant discourses of autonomy and subjective self-determination. Žižek's work added to this the element, present everywhere in Lacan's work but sometimes lacking from his commentators, of an intensely stimulating dialogue with an extensive psychoanalytic, philosophical and literary tradition. In this respect, it is a significant fact that Žižek never came to Lacan directly — he is too young to have sat through the seminars whose power we can now judge only in written form — but through the seminars and teaching of Jacques-Alain Miller.

The emphasis of Žižek's later work has moved away from the sort of exposition of the work of Lacan via various fields that, if it were possible to use the term purely descriptively rather than as a proper name, might be called cultural studies. The genre of the 'everything you want to know about Lacan explained by other means' that marked his early books has given way to a more programmatic analysis of philosophy, of religion and of politics and society that, while grounded in the Lacanian framework, has nevertheless other aims that are more overtly philosophical and political. In retrospect, these aims have always been present and his more recent work indicates not so much a shift as a shift of emphasis. The emphasis on political and social dimensions, in particular, is not such a common thing in psychoanalysis, for while it is true that there has been no shortage of political engagement, this has typically taken the form of an add-on to the clinical practice of psychoanalysis itself. From the other side, critical theorists, social theorists and cultural theorists have looked to psychoanalysis for what it can contribute to an already more or less clearly defined and well articulated position. This has tended to make for an optimistic reading of psychoanalysis which, though by no means universal, argues for a reinterpretation in progressive terms of what are standardly seen as the conservative implications of psychoanalytic theory.[2]

Žižek's political analysis thus arises directly from psychoanalysis of a Lacanian orientation. His is, to be sure, just one approach that could be taken, fundamentally marked as it is by a Hegelianism acquired at an earlier stage. But in my view this Hegelianism is pre-Oedipal in the true Lacanian sense; it leaves a trace that has been reconfigured *nachträglichkeit*, and the essential aspect of Žižek's work is clearly Lacanian.

While this approach, in which political considerations are filtered through the lens of psychoanalysis, is not the least interesting aspect of Žižek's work, it also raises some real questions. Žižek has not shied away from these, and indeed has taken the challenge up to recent criticisms which have claimed that psychoanalysis has something inherently conservative about it. In the context of this important debate about the political implications of psychoanalysis, and of the Lacanian orientation in particular, there is a question that arises with respect to Žižek's account of both individual action and political change. This question concerns what Žižek calls acts of 'total' or 'absolute' freedom. The concept of act of absolute freedom, as I shall call it, plays a key role in his work because it is central to his account of how individuals or groups can intervene to bring about significant political or social change. I will discuss first Žižek's account, then the role it plays for him, and finally I will discuss some of the reservations that I have about it.

According to Žižek an act of absolute freedom can be performed either by individuals or groups — the structure or 'logic' is the same in either case. Essentially, for Žižek absolute freedom addresses the issue whether everything that happens or that one can do is determined in advance by a kind of monolithic big Other. On Žižek's view, not only is it the case that what practices are authorized is determined by the Other, but also all so-called 'subversive' practices that challenge and supposedly undermine the dominant code in actual fact themselves turn out to be determined by and in a sense even authorized by the code and thus fail in their subversive aim. For an act to be truly subversive it must break with the code in a more radical or fundamental, or even absolute, way and Žižek's concept of an *act* of absolute freedom, which he says derives from the concept of act in Lacan's work, is intended to capture this idea of an absolute break.

In his *Enjoy Your Symptom!* Žižek takes the 'irresolution' of the ending of Rossellini's film *Stromboli* as an opportunity to discuss this notion of an act of absolute freedom — or at least, the subjective dimension of such an act.[3] The film ends with Karin, having fled her husband and the suffocating life of the small village which for a number of years she has made her home, reaching the region of the island's volcanic crater where she is overcome by fumes. As she begins to lose consciousness she negates — says 'No' to — her adoptive community, but then, for a brief moment, she awakens to some sort of epiphanic experience in which the dour grimness of the island life has been transformed in her own appreciation of its eerie beauty. As Žižek stresses, the ending of the film leaves fundamentally indeterminate the subsequent step that Karin will take: return to or flight from the village. At least, this is how things unfold in its Italian version, for by the artifice of a voiceover the American version leaves us in no doubt that Karin finds reconciliation with life in the village. Žižek clearly considers the American version a mistake because, he says, it is extremely important that, and this is a point made by Rossellini, Karin's *act* of renunciation should not be confused with any *action* she might subsequently carry out.

By this very irresolution of its ending, *Stromboli* marks the proper dimension of the act: it ends at the precise point at which the *act* is already accomplished, although no *action* is yet performed. The act done (or more appropriately: endured) by Karin is that of *symbolic suicide*: an act of 'losing all,' of withdrawing from symbolic reality, that enables us to begin anew from the 'zero point,' from that point of absolute freedom called by Hegel 'abstract negativity' (1992, 43; as henceforth all the page references).

For Žižek the subjective dimension of this act of absolute freedom portrayed in the film is that what had once been experienced as a loss or renunciation becomes transformed into the 'loss of a loss itself,' or the renunciation of a renunciation: that is, what 'a moment ago, [Karin] was afraid to lose' in fact comes to be totally lacking in value and significance for her, and she thus becomes aware that, despite what her fears may once have been, she can lose nothing (43). This act, which is an '*act* in the Lacanian sense,' is an act of 'withdrawal by means of which we *renounce renunciation itself,* [and become] aware of the fact that we have nothing to lose in a loss' (43).

This renunciation of renunciation is what distinguishes Karin's 'symbolic suicide,' as Žižek calls it, from 'actual suicide'. In actual suicide the act 'remains caught within the network of symbolic communication: by killing himself the subject attempts to send a message to the Other, i.e., it is an act that functions as [for instance] an acknowledgement of guilt, a sobering warning, a pathetic appeal' (44). By contrast, an act of symbolic suicide 'aims to exclude the subject from the very intersubjective circuit' (44).

This redoubled renunciation, 'renunciation of renunciation' or 'loss of loss,' is then a defining characteristic of an act of radical freedom. A second, equally important aspect is that an act 'radically transforms its ... agent': 'After an act, I'm literally "not the same as before"' (44). The subject is 'annihilated and subsequently reborn'; 'the act involves a kind of ... *aphanisis* of the subject' (44). This aphanisis occurs because of the cut with all prior symbolic moorings by means of which the subject has acquired all previous identity. A *new* symbolic network entails the 'death' of the old and the 'birth' of a new subject.

Note at this point that these two features of 'an act' — the rebirth of the subject and the realization that henceforth there is nothing to fear, that nothing can harm one — are ways in which religious conversion and faith have been described and give a corresponding religious tone to Žižek's notion of an act. While I wonder whether this is accidental, or incidental, this is an impression created by the fact that we have so far considered merely the subjective dimension of the issue.

We should also note that notions of radical transformation of the subject are notoriously vague as to their political or practical consequences. We know that in religious metaphors of rebirth or in more epistemological functions as in, for instance, Cartesian subjective enlightenment, while the subject is in some sense totally reborn — nothing is the same, everything is changed — this rebirth may well be achieved with no immediate or obvious or even any real change of any practical kind. This has been noted by numerous commentators a propos of Cartesian *askesis* in the *Meditations*, just as it has been noted concerning meditative experiences properly so-called. In purely subjective transformation there is no implication that there will ever be real practical consequences for the lives of people involved; an act of absolute freedom need not result in any practical change. It can, in an important sense, leave everything as it is. Yet, while it *may* leave everything as it is, it may not either. The very example Lacan initially chose to introduce the quilting point, which is the High Priest's 'fear of God' in Racine's *Athaliah*, indicates the subject's anchorage in a symbolic system that not only sustains his resolve in the face of mortal danger but also converts the irresolute Abner to the cause.

To see the political dimension of the act, in which the *status quo ante* is irremediably destroyed, we need to consider its objective effects, which include on the one hand the act's consequences specifically for the agent, and on the other the act's consequences in a broader sense.

In both cases the consequences of an act are radically underdetermined. Thus, the subjective rebirth Žižek speaks of goes along with the fact that an act is 'radically *unaccountable*,' and that one can never fully *foresee its consequences*, in particular, 'the way it will transform the existing symbolic space' (45). In an act one is risking everything and putting everything at stake, oneself, one's symbolic identity, included. It is a 'rupture after which "nothing remains the same"' (45). And this is, moreover, invoked to explain why we can never foresee the way in which history will unfold in advance, but can only explain its course retrospectively.

Furthermore, 'the act is . . . always a "crime"', or a ' "transgression" . . . of the limit of the symbolic community' to which one belongs. (44) Though this is not stated in as many words, the reason for this would appear to be that from the standpoint of the current symbolic Other the act is essentially both destructive and gratuitous. Thus, Žižek states that an act is always *negative*, an act is always 'an act of annihilation, of wiping out — we not only don't know what will come of it, its final outcome is ultimately even insignificant, strictly secondary in relation to the NO! of the pure act' (44). It is fairly easy to see then that an act achieves what subversive practices cannot, namely, a rupture with the big Other.

Finally, Žižek considers that it is no accident that the paradigmatic example of an act, which he takes to be Antigone's 'No!' to Creon, is the act of a woman. And he wonders whether the genuine act is '*feminine*,' in contrast with the masculine performative that is the founding gesture of a new order. From this point of view the

difference masculine/feminine no longer coincides with that of active/passive, spiritual/sensual, culture/nature, etc. The very masculine *activity* is already an escape from the abysmal dimension of the feminine *act*. The 'break with nature' is on the side of woman, and man's compulsive activity is ultimately nothing but a desperate attempt to repair the traumatic incision of this rupture' (46).

In a further development that appears later in *Enjoy Your Symptom!*
Žižek equates the genuine act with the authentic ethical act, as this
is understood by Lacan. Such an act 'presents the only moment
when we are effectively "free": Antigone is "free" after she has been
excommunicated from the community'. (77) And Žižek suggests that
acts similar to Antigone's today are typically dubbed 'terrorist,' 'like
the gesture of Gudrun Ensslin, leader of the "Red Army Faction", a
Maoist "terrorist" organization, who killed herself in the maximum
security prison in 1978,' where what was 'really disturbing ... was
not the bombs but the refusal of the forced choice, of the fundamental
social pact' (76–7). Insisting upon this radical nature of Antigone's act,
Žižek adds that 'today, when Antigone is as a rule "domesticated",
made into a pathetic guardian of the community against tyrannical
state power, it is all the more necessary to insist upon the scandalous
character of her "No!" to Creon: those who do not want to talk about
the "terrorist" Gudrun, should also keep quiet about Antigone'. (77)
Thus, far from reproaching the RAF for going too far when they
suspended even elementary ethical principles, we should acknowledge
that their 'suspension of the ethical' is the refusal of the subject's
alienation in a universal symbolic pact (78).

It is important for Žižek's purposes that Antigone's act not just lie
outside the law but that it be a complete rupture with the law. Yet the
comparison with Ensslinn is surely pushed too far. In both cases, to be
sure, there is a no-saying to the state power just as there is a similarity
in their suicidal act. And it is also true that Antigone is no 'guardian of
the community' since her act is blind to the consequences it may have
for those amongst whom she lives and presumably, though there is
little evidence of this in the play, for whom she cares. But it does not
follow that what was 'really disturbing about the [Red Army Faction]
"terrorism" was not the bombs but the refusal of the forced choice,
of the fundamental social pact' (77–8). On the contrary, it is precisely
the campaign of terror that distinguishes the Red Army Faction from
Antigone, who is no terrorist but a person who refuses to comply
with a command she thinks is wrong — and who does so, moreover,
in the name of a higher law.

Indeed, I think that Žižek is too quick to lump together cases
that are actually different in important ways. Not only are Antigone
and Ensslinn different cases but so too are Antigone and Sygne de
Coûfontaine whom Žižek also compares with one another. I argue
below that Antigone's act is *not* an act of absolute freedom in the
required sense. It is arguable that Sygne de Coûfontaine's act is, but

not Antigone's. And the reason why Antigone's is not is that she is acting, and sacrificing herself, blindly, in the name of the law — even if it is the fractured law of Oedipus.

Žižek's notion of an act has an important role to play in his response in *The Ticklish Subject* to a criticism Judith Butler makes of psychoanalysis. This response occurs in the context of a defence of Lacan against the criticism that his views allow no possibility of resistance to the existing power structure because, as Butler argues in *The Psychic Life of Power*, all resistance 'presumes the continuation of the law' and thus 'contributes to its status quo'.[4] If this is so, then all 'resistance appears doomed to perpetual defeat' (*Psychic Life*, 88).

Žižek's response is to claim that Butler has got Lacan wrong. Indeed, for Lacan, 'radical rearticulation of the predominant symbolic Order is altogether possible — this is what his *point de capiton* (...) is about: when a new *point de capiton* emerges, the socio-symbolic field is not only displaced, its very structuring principle changes' (262). Thus, 'Lacan leaves open the possibility of a radical rearticulation of the entire symbolic field by means of an *act* proper, a passage through "symbolic death"' (262). And this, he claims, is the whole point of Lacan's reading of *Antigone*:

Antigone (...) risks her entire social existence, defying the socio-symbolic power of the City embodied in (...) Creon (...). For Lacan, there is no ethical act proper without taking the risk of such a 'momentary suspension of the big Other' (...); an authentic act occurs only when the subject risks a gesture that is no longer 'covered up' by the big Other. (263–4)

Butler's point that for psychoanalysis opposition to the law is merely its acknowledgement and preservation by other means mirrors an old one made within psychoanalysis itself, dating back to Freud whose account of the primal horde captures what is at issue: the brothers' revolt against the father merely reinforces their own subjugation to his law.[5] And don't we all know, from Lacan's public pronouncements, that he endorses this view himself? His contemporary criticism of the French student revolution in which he referred to the *mois*, egos/months, of May, and his accusation that they were in search of a master whom, moreover, they would no doubt find is a *prima facie* indication that all revolt acts within and confirms the law whose chains it thinks it is breaking. The point is — isn't it? — that revolt is structural. For while structures do not march in the streets, they determine who will: how, then, can resistance lead to radical change?

Žižek is in general agreement that real social change is no easy matter. He says, on the one hand, that there can be 'imaginary' resistance to the symbolic order which is a 'misrecognition of the symbolic network that determines us' (262) and, on the other, that Butler is both too optimistic and too pessimistic from a Lacanian point of view. Her optimism stems from her overestimation of 'the subversive potential of disturbing the functioning of the big Other through the practice of performative reconfiguration [and] displace-ment' — optimism because such practices 'ultimately support what they intend to subvert, since the very field of such "transgressions" is already taken into account (. . .) by the (. . .) big Other' which includes both 'symbolic norms *and* their codified transgressions' (264). On the other hand, her pessimism does not allow for the radically subversive 'act' that is capable of producing a 'thorough restructuring of the hegemonic symbolic order in its totality' (264). Whereas Butler insists that any 'protest' imitates the law it claims to overthrow and that the hegemonic symbolic order can only be subverted by marginal gestures of displacement, Žižek counterclaims that the *act*, which defies and says 'No!' to the big Other, is the sole event capable of producing a complete reconfiguration of the symbolic order itself.

Thus we can see that the *act* of which Žižek speaks assumes, and indeed must assume, considerable importance for him in the context of change. The constraining effects of the prevailing social order are manifest not just in subjective compliance with its imperatives but also in the 'subversive' acts that transgress its norms. Yet from the point of view of political change there would also appear to be a very disturbing implication of this view of an act: its radical indeterminacy, which implies that *all* political action is gratuitous and gratuitous in an absolute sense — not just from the point of the present order but gratuitous *per se*. To see this, let me pursue further Žižek's, and Lacan's, treatment of *Antigone*, which can be taken as something of a paradigm case.

For Žižek's purposes it is important that Antigone's act lie outside the law. But is this really so? While I can agree that Antigone's refusal, her 'No!' to Creon, is fundamentally indeterminate, and that such is the nature of the *point de capiton* in general, her action is not a lawless one, nor is it beyond the symbolic world. Thus, while the cases of Antigone and Ensslin have some obvious parallels, there are fundamental differences: it is an extremely important feature of Antigone's act that it be nothing other than a no-saying. Her opposition is mute and stubborn, she may well be indifferent to the consequences of her act for her city, she does not attempt to overthrow or subvert Creon's law, no actual attempt is made to destroy his city, which is also her city, for she knows that there is a 'higher law' in the name of which she acts. In this respect she is more like Luther who, with his 'Here I stand and can do no other,' is resolute in the knowledge that he is doing God's will. Furthermore, the reason that she is more like Luther is that her motivation comes from her obedience to the law of the Father.

It is true that Antigone makes a choice: she chooses death and, as Lacan observes, in choosing death she is choosing to be the guardian of the being of the criminal as such. Is this choice one of radical freedom? Or shall we say, at least assuming for a moment that she is not a character in a play, that her choice is a neurotic choice and, moreover, that she is seriously neurotic. If we are prepared to look at Antigone from this point of view, then it seems to me that the 'clinical case' of Antigone was demonstrated by Freud in his *Studies on Hysteria* with Anna O., a young woman devoted to the ideals of the father and to sacrificing herself, her own desires, to the perpetuation of the Oedipus complex. Just as Antigone does.

There is a difference, though. While the character in the play acts entirely on her own and neither seeks nor requires assistance of any kind, Anna O., the neurotic, has her symptoms. She complains about them and they lead her to seek help. This is part of what is meant by hysteria: in their symptoms men and women will refuse a sacrifice they have made in the Name-of-the-Father — a point easier to consider in the light of Lacan's subsequent clarification of his position on the Name-of-the-Father, when, in *Seminar 17*, he situates the aim of analysis beyond the Oedipus complex. Since in the case of Antigone we are not dealing with a clinical situation organized in order to give analytic form to symptoms, we can't really treat it in the way we would treat a case. But we have known since Freud that it is very common for the hysteric, despite his or her complaints, to manifest a desire to sustain the father's desire more than their own. This is something that can extend a long way. As we know, for example from the clinic of anorexics, it can extend to the point of death.

If we consider Antigone in this way, then, if we compare her to a case, we might say that at the initial point at which she refuses Creon she best resembles an hysterical young woman. For she is a woman who, when dreadful contingencies in her life catch her in a situation in which she is forced to make a decision, decides somewhat blindly. If I am right in this, then the important question to ask is in what sense Antigone is acting on her desire and, consequently, whether her 'act' can be described in the way Žižek sees it.

For if it is true that Antigone is 'acting on her desire' we have to consider what this means. The first thing to notice is that while throughout the play she is, apparently, acting upon her desire, it is her *conscious* desire that is at stake. At no point is there any reflection upon, wonder about, doubt or rumination over, no analysis of what her desire is. She's always and constantly acting upon her desire and is oblivious to what drives her. The second thing to notice is that if there is any moment at which she can be said 'not to have given ground over her desire,' as Lacan puts it in *Seminar VII*, it comes when she has passed beyond the point of acceptance of her death sentence.[6] Now, if she has not given ground with respect to her desire, this is far from being a moment at which she has gone beyond the Other in an act of absolute freedom; it is rather a moment in which she recognizes what she has been for the Other and she has accepted it.

Moreover, the pathos of the tragedy of *Antigone* draws our attention to a particular type of relation to desire that tends, owing to its inherent and structural unsatisfaction — a desire for an unsatisfied desire — to go beyond the limits of everything, but especially, here, beyond the limits of the person's own ideals. This is hysterical desire. And if psychoanalysis can speak of 'hysterical desire' it is because one can distinguish between the hysteric's and the obsessional's desire. This is why Hamlet appears as an example of the depressive obsessional, whereas Antigone presents as the epitome of manic hysterical behaviour; whereas Hamlet has become the prisoner of the figure of an ideal father, Antigone has become a hero of, a martyr to, the father's desire.

This is why for Lacan the turning point in *Antigone* is the point at which Antigone becomes aware of and moved by the loss she has experienced. It is not the point when she decides, 'I will bury my brother,' and says 'No!' to Creon. At this point, whatever she may believe her desire to be, it is in fact a conscious decision that is an expression of her symptom, which is her tendency to sacrifice and to act in conformity with her family destiny. This means that, of her desire, Antigone might say something like: 'I have been the eyes of my blind father. I have been his most beloved treasure and as dear to him as his own gaze — this gaze which represents his crime. Moreover, I have been this crime myself'.

This at least is how things stand at the outset, on the occurrence of her initial no-saying to Creon. Note however that there is a subsequent crucial moment in the play. It plays the role of a certain *capitonnage*, quilting, that retroactively determines the meaning of Antigone's initial act. It is only *after* she has come to accept what her written destiny has been and what the signifiers of this destiny are that she can also accept some loss in her identification — hence her lamentation. It is only at the time of this lament, when she is 'between two deaths' and *still* chooses to do it because she knows that it *is* her fate and that she has accepted it after all, that we can say she has abandoned the ideals of her life and that she can be considered as belonging to a field beyond the pleasure principle.

Initially the situation is constructed in such a way that she is forced to choose between two alternatives. Either bury her brother or give ground over her desire. The loss of ideals that is described at the second moment, the renunciation and abandonment of her feminine ideals specially, allows her to transform what had been a symptomatic position into a new relationship to her womanhood. She moves from a position in which she *incarnated* the Oedipal object to a point at which she consents to be an object in a different way — someone, at least in principle, capable of loving and being loved and, at least in principle, capable of having a child. Thus at this point she sees herself not only as a daughter — and I think this explains the puzzling point about the loss of a brother and the loss of a husband — but as a virtual bride and a virtual mother. At this moment she formulates, for the first time, an idea of what her accomplishments as a woman might have been. Even as she realizes what she has lost — this is very important and is emphasized by Lacan — in spite of this acceptance she still decides to realize and enact her destiny in all its consequences.

In summary, then, the general point I would like to make about Antigone's 'act' is that far from creating the absolute freedom Žižek refers to, her initial 'No!' to Creon is entirely consistent with, and binds her to, her family destiny and paternal law. Her 'No,' which is an act of both defiance and sacrifice, is initially quite ambiguous in its status; she defies the law of her city in the name of her (Oedipal) law — a law to which, by the very same act, she defiantly sacrifices herself. Indeed, this ambiguity *is* resolved but only in the second moment when she renounces her ideals and seals her fate. But this second moment *also* entails the recognition and acknowledgement of those ideals. To my mind there is no 'loss of loss' but a late *acknowledgement* of her loss even as she *renounces* her ideals.

There is a similarity here with the aim of a psychoanalysis, which is to take the subject to the point where he or she discovers what the law of his or her destiny has been. This is a point that in *Seminar VII* Lacan makes in the following way: 'This law is in the first place always the acceptance of something that began to be articulated before him in previous generations, and which is strictly speaking *Até*' (300). Thus, Lacan makes the claim, and it is one that applies to Antigone, *both* that the subject is the result of the Other's desire, *and* that there is an acceptance of this on the part of the subject. In psychoanalytic treatment we are not dealing with something completely automatic. There is choice required by the subject. This choice always involves the *acceptance* of what Lacan describes as an *Até*. Even if this *Até* 'does not always reach the tragic level of Antigone's *Até*, it is nevertheless 'closely related to misfortune' (300).

In the case of Antigone, as elsewhere, we should distinguish between a desire for death and the death drive. In this case, and in others too, they may well correspond. This is not in dispute. But Lacan is more interested in showing how the death drive can enter someone's life than he is in any pure desire for death. But we can also say that a pure desire will always be a pure desire for death. In fact in Lacan's subsequent work — in the final pages of *Seminar XI* specifically — we find the claim that there is no such thing as a pure desire that is not a desire for death.[7]

I mention this point because I believe that Žižek has a somewhat idealized view of desire. And I think that to consider properly Lacan's position on Antigone's desire and on her sacrifice, which means not idealizing the whimsical and gratuitous aspect of either, we should draw upon these last pages of Lacan's 1964 *Seminar XI*, which cast a different light on the case of Antigone discussed in 1960 in *Seminar VII*. Lacan makes some comments in support of the view that the exaltation of desire and its occasional confusion with whimsical behaviour a propos of the case of Antigone can mislead us seriously about the ethics of psychoanalysis. Lacan puts it thus, 'The offering to obscure gods of an object of sacrifice is something to which few subjects can resist succumbing, as if under some monstrous spell (. . .). There are certainly few who do not succumb to the fascination of the sacrifice in itself' (275). Alongside Antigone we can place Kant as a philosopher who has the idea of a pure desire. And, as in the case of Antigone, Kant's ethics entails a secret jouissance of sacrifice — a point well made by Žižek in fact.

There is a further indication relevant to Lacan's thoughts about this 'pure desire' in these last pages of *Seminar XI* when he also warns us that desire in its pure state culminates in the sacrifice, strictly speaking, of everything that is the object of love in one's human tenderness. Not only the rejection of the pathological object, in Kant's sense of 'pathological,' but also its sacrifice and its murder. So, from this point of view in which we take Lacan's views of four years later into account, I think that the sum of Lacan's considerations about Antigone, about her desire, about how far she is beyond everyone and does not give ground over her desire, are not to be seen as an endorsement or exaltation of this 'pure desire'.

To summarize Žižek's position, as I see it, central to his analysis of political action is the concept of an act of absolute freedom. And the key to this concept is the notion of a rupture with the big Other: any practice that does not rupture with the big Other will be condemned to repeat one or other of the practices made possible by the Other itself, which remains unaltered and unthreatened as a result. Thus, the only practice that can rupture with the big Other is one that has the characteristics of an act, as outlined above.

Now, the question that this raises is how radical this rupture needs to be to ensure a transformation of the big Other. And here it strikes me that Žižek is faced with an undesirable dilemma. On the one hand, the act needs to be grounded in a radical no-saying that is inexplicable not just in terms of a given big Other, but in terms of *any other Other whatsoever*. This is because the act of absolute freedom, as Žižek understands it, derives its essential features (its freedom, its gratuitousness, its criminality, its unaccountability and unpredictability) from the fact that it lies outside all possible symbolic dimensions. It strikes me that not only does Antigone not conform to this requirement but also that it makes an act indistinguishable from mere whimsicality. There is no objective criterion and there can clearly be no appeal to any subjective features to distinguish an act of absolute freedom from a gratuitous act. On the other hand, an act of absolute freedom may be free relative to a given symbolic order. This of course makes freedom relative rather than absolute — relative to a particular form, or determination, of the Other. It will be free from *its* strictures, gratuitous from *its* point of view, criminal in *its* eyes, and perhaps unaccountable and unpredictable within *its* framework. But it is unclear whether it is capable of doing the work that Žižek wants it to do: namely to provide the means of rupture with a given framework.

Finally, I think that Žižek is inclined to overestimate how radical Antigone's act actually is, at least in terms of it being an absolute no-saying or refusal. I think it is improbable that her act is an act of absolute freedom in the required sense because, as discussed above, her no-saying reveals an allegiance to the autochthonous law of the father that is the source of her motivation. I see little ground for 'absolute freedom' in this act.

RUSSELL GRIGG
Deakin University

NOTES

1 Slavoj Žižek, *The Sublime Object of Ideology* (London: Verso, 1989).
2 See the recent Ph.D. thesis by Craig Smith in Psychoanalytic Studies at Deakin University, *Psychoanalysis and Social Transformation*.
3 Slavoj Žižek, *Enjoy Your Symptom!* (New York and London: Routledge, 1992).
4 Judith Butler, *The Psychic Life of Power* (Stanford, CA: Stanford University Press, 1997), p. 88.
5 Butler's recent *Antigone's Claim* (New York: Columbia University Press, 2000) adds little to this question of absolute freedom directly and, though interesting on other counts, will not be discussed here.
6 Jacques Lacan, *The Seminar of Jacques Lacan, Book VII, The Ethics of Psychoanalysis, 1959–1960*, edited by Jacques-Alain Miller, translated by Dennis Porter (New York: Norton, 1992).
7 Jacques Lacan, *The Four Fundamental Concepts of Psychoanalysis*, edited by Jacques-Alain Miller, translated by Alan Sheridan (Harmondsworth: Penguin, 1979).

Žižek, religion and ideology

There is sometimes much to be learned from a thinker's more apparently tangential sources, who seem to have no direct connexion with his or her major intellectual reference points. By the same token, there is something to be gleaned from a thinker's choice of analogies. Žižek is famed for the aplomb with which he juxtaposes abstruse points of philosophical or psychoanalytic theory with examples from cinema or popular culture. But religious analogies occur with perhaps surprising frequency throughout his work. In his recent work, the scope of religion has expanded so that the analogical digression has become the substance of an argument. There is some point then in addressing these issues conjointly, by examining the use of religious writers and themes both in earlier and in very recent works of Žižek's.[1]

Althusser, Pascal and the theory of ideology

The presence of Althusser in Žižek's work is hardly surprising: a Marxist with Lacanian inclinations seems an obvious guest at Žižek's symposia. If we knew that a friend of his had been invited to keep him company, we would have a pretty good guess who that would be. Althusser repeatedly cited Spinoza as an inspiration, and two of his major followers, Etienne Balibar and Pierre Macherey, have done important work on Spinoza.[2] But instead we would find Pascal. Instead of the arch-heretic who denied the existence of a personal God, and preached this-worldly happiness through the exercise of reason, we find an apologist for Christianity, whose affiliations were with the Jansenist movement, a hard-line tendency in Roman Catholicism with a pessimistic view of human nature and a rigorous doctrine of predestination.

A reader as attentive as Žižek, however, would hardly have overlooked the presence of Pascal at the centre of Althusser's essay on the theory of ideology. (Years later, on re-reading Pascal, Althusser recognised him as the source of the whole theory.)[3] Žižek prolongs the Althusserian enterprise by using Pascal to explore the nature of belief, in ways that go beyond Althusser himself.

Althusser's main use of Pascal in the essay on ideology is to invert the hierarchical ordering of belief and action. The common conception, or ideology, holds that the individual should act according to his or her beliefs. For Althusser, action precedes belief: the ideas in which an individual believes *are* his or her acts, inserted into material practices regulated by material rituals laid down by the ideological apparatus in question. And the inspiration for this inversion is Pascal, whom he paraphrases as follows: 'Kneel, move your lips in prayer, and you will believe' (pp. 41–3).[4] Žižek's approach is rather different. He begins his Pascalian excursus with another fragment not mentioned by Althusser, but recognized by Pascalian interpreters as vital.

For we must make no mistake about ourselves: we are as much automaton as mind (...). Proofs only convince the mind; habit provides the strongest proofs, and those that are most believed. It inclines the automaton, which leads the mind unconsciously along with it.[5]

Žižek reads 'automaton' as denoting the 'automatism of the signifier, of the symbolic network in which the subjects are caught,' and comments as follows: 'Here Pascal produces the very Lacanian definition of the unconscious: "the automaton (i.e. the dead, senseless letter) which leads the mind unconsciously (...) with it"' (*SOI*, 37). Now at first sight this looks like a simple misreading, or perhaps a joke. The standard gloss of Pascal's use of the term 'automaton' is that it denotes the body.[6] (This is basically how Althusser reads Pascal: the performance of bodily rituals subjects the individual to the ideological state apparatus that prescribes the ritual.) I am not primarily concerned here to show that Žižek's reading of Pascal is sound or unsound — there are certainly points the specialist would contest. But although the identification of the automaton with the letter of the unconscious seems far-fetched, it should not be altogether written off. Another major Pascal scholar, Philippe Sellier, takes Pascal's concept of the automaton to cover not only the body, but part of our psychic life.[7] This brings us a little nearer to Žižek in that it allows us to see not merely the body but also the unconscious as involved in the production of belief. As Žižek observes:

What distinguishes this Pascalian 'custom' from insipid behaviourist wisdom (...) is the paradoxical status of a *belief before belief*: by following a custom, the subject believes without knowing it, so that the final conversion is merely a formal act by means of which we recognize what have already believed. In other words, what the behaviourist reading of Pascalian 'custom' misses is the crucial fact that the external custom is always a material support for the subject's unconscious (*SOI*, 40).

Elsewhere, he analyses the Althusserian-Pascalian theory as follows:

The implicit logic of [the] argument is: kneel down and *you shall believe that you knelt down because of your belief* — that is, your following the ritual is an expression/effect of your inner belief; in short, the 'external' ritual performatively generates its own ideological foundation.[8]

There is none the less an important shift here from Althusser's concerns. Althusser's point was that in all ideology there is a subjection that can be conceived on the lines of Pascal's model of conversion, but that does not always take the subjective form of conversion. Conversion is the special case that reveals the general law. He uses Pascalian theory to bolster the Marxist theory of ideology, but makes no analogy between religious conversion and political commitment. Žižek explicitly does (*SOI*, pp. 39–43). That is to say, he is much more alert to the ethical issue of how political commitment is to be grounded or justified. This emerges from his analysis of another fragment of Pascal's:

Custom is the whole of equity for the sole reason that it is accepted. That is the mystic basis of its authority. Anyone who tries to bring it back to its first principles destroys it.[9]

Žižek reads this as implying that belief can never be objectively justified by rational argument. One submits to it in the same way as, according to Pascal in the same fragment, we submit to law: because it is law. 'We must search for rational reasons which can substantiate our belief (. . .) but (. . .) these reasons reveal themselves only to those who already believe' (*SOI*, 37).[10] That is to say, belief, or submission to the Law, must be understood in relation to the concept of the superego, that is, 'an injunction which is experienced as traumatic, "senseless" — that is, which cannot be integrated into the symbolic universe of the subject' (p. 37); while on the other hand, this traumatic fact must be 'repressed into the unconscious, through the ideological, imaginary experience of the "meaning" of the Law, of its foundation in Justice, Truth (or, in a more modern way, functionality)' (p. 38). The section of the wager fragment to which Althusser alludes, in which Pascal urges the unbelieving would-be believer to follow religious rituals, is thus quoted at length in support of the thesis of the primacy of belief over the reasons that vindicate it — for the believer (pp. 38–9).

This assimilation of belief to Pascal's concept of law and custom enables Žižek to plug the gaps in Althusserian theory. Althusser failed to show how the Ideological State Apparatuses produce the effect of recognition and subjection. But if the law is obeyed, not because it is right, but because it is law, and we adhere to it *because we cannot justify it*, then its power to subject seems more comprehensible: 'This external "machine" of State Apparatuses exercises its force only insofar as it is experienced, in the unconscious economy of the subject, as a traumatic senseless injunction' (p. 43). We learn, further, from Pascal that the internalization of the symbolic machine of ideology never fully succeeds, 'that there is always a residue, a leftover, a strain of traumatic irrationality and senselessness sticking to it, and that *this leftover, far from hindering the full submission of the subject to the ideological command, is the very condition of it*' (p. 43). Why this is so is explained by another reference to Pascal (though also to Descartes). Ideological commitment produces various effects but only when they are sought as a by-product. Thus Pascal promises (*Pensées*, fragment 418) that religious faith will produce terrestrial advantages, in that it will improve our moral character and offer pleasures that provide an alternative to those we have given up. 'But the point is,' as Žižek observes, 'that I can achieve this terrestrial profit only if I really believe in God' (*SOI*, 83). Pascal has dangerously revealed the 'enjoyment which is at work in ideology, in the ideological renunciation itself' (p. 84).[11]

Pascal's theory of law is invoked again in *For They Know Not What They Do*. Power depends on the belief that the law is authentic and eternal, but this conceals its real foundations:

'At the beginning' of the law, there is a certain 'outlaw,' a certain Real of violence which coincides with the act itself of the establishment of the reign of law: the ultimate truth about the reign of law is that of an usurpation, and all classical politico-philosophical thought rests on the disavowal of this violent act of foundation. (p. 204)[12]

A theory of belief originally designed to support religion has been diverted to other purposes. But this is not surprising. The theory, it could be argued, has no intrinsic theological content. Pascal was concerned with the mechanism of belief, which works irrespective of its object (custom determines also our non-religious beliefs, attaches us to this-worldly goals and values — religious rituals are first and foremost a counterweight to this). Likewise, Pascal's critical insight into law and society can be linked to his Jansenism: the theological insistence on the absence of God from the everyday world has to be vindicated by a relentless 'demystifying' critique. But the demystification can be accepted without its positive counterpart, the development of a Christian reading of history.

Grace and predestination

The situation is slightly different in Žižek's more recent work. For here we find explicitly theological concepts being invoked to theorize the condition of the subject, as if without them the modern predicament of choice could not be analysed.

This can be seen if we begin on a non-theological terrain. In *The Ticklish Subject* Žižek sets out to defend Hegel against the criticism that he makes all particularity dissolve in the all-encompassing self-realization of an Absolute Subject that reconciles all oppositions (p. 76). To this end, he recapitulates the Hegelian account of the subject's self-constitution through the affirmation of universality. Hegel, says Žižek, was the first to elaborate 'the properly modern notion of individualization through secondary identification': one becomes an autonomous individual only by tearing oneself away from one's primordial 'organic' community, and recognizing the substance of one's being in another, secondary, *universal*, community. Where in the name of this universal one renounces one's primary identifications, we have 'abstract' universality; when they are reintegrated, 'concrete' universality (p. 90). But 'concrete' universality can never occur as direct identification with a concrete whole: 'in every direct choice between abstract negativity and a concrete whole, the subject has to choose abstract negativity' (p. 95). In other words, to perform 'an excessive, unilateral gesture which throws the harmonious order of the Whole out of balance (. . .) an exercise of utter caprice based on no good reason' is 'the only Way for the Universal to assert itself "for itself", against all determinate particular content' (p. 96). He insists that for Hegel no particular content can ever embody the universal it seeks adequately to embody. (For example, the affirmation of the universal value of an ethnic identity as that which binds 'all of us' together against some oppressor will be found always to exclude some of the population it purports to unify.) In this sense, there is a gap and/or excess constitutive of every established order (p. 113).

For this reason, there can be no solution to the ethical dilemmas of modernity in any return to identification with an organic community. Since no established order or tradition can ground our allegiance, the characteristic modern choice has something irreducibly gratuitous about it. It is thus akin to religious commitment: for Kierkegaard, Žižek suggests, '*religion is eminently modern*: the traditional universe is ethical, while the Religious involves a radical disruption of the old ways — true religion is a crazy wager on the Impossible we have to make once we lose support in tradition' (p. 115). The mention of the wager is designed to remind us of the exemplary position of Pascal at this interface between religion and the emergence of modernity. The Christian tradition thus provides Žižek with a model that leftism cannot dispense with: a renewed Left, he says, should fully endorse the Kierkegaardian claim of the modernity of Christianity (p. 211). Kierkegaard goes beyond the antithesis between inner sentiment and empty outward ritual: true religion is more internal, in that faith cannot be adequately externalized through language, and more external: 'when I truly believe,' Žižek explains, 'I accept that the source of my faith is not in myself; that in some inexplicable way, it comes from outside, from God Himself — in His grace, God addressed me, it was not I who raised myself to Him' (p. 211). Something analogous is proposed by psychoanalysis: not the rediscovery of an inner truth, but the accession to a new symbolic configuration of one's being (p. 212).

'Grace' becomes a recurrent figure in Žižek's analysis of choice. Thus, in the course of a critical but sympathetic exposition of Heidegger, he discusses Heidegger's conception of the decision by which an individual, or more especially a people, assumes a destiny — not a free choice between alternatives but 'the choice of "freely assuming" one's imposed destiny' (p. 18).

Žižek comments as follows:

> This paradox, necessary if one is to avoid the vulgar liberal notion of freedom of choice, indicates the theological problematic of *predestination* and *Grace*: a true decision/choice ([...] the fundamental choice by means of which I 'choose myself') presupposes that I assume a passive attitude of 'letting myself be chosen' — in short, *free choice and Grace are strictly equivalent.*
>
> (p. 18: Žižek's italics)

Lest we take him to be dealing with 'an obscurantist-theological problematic' Žižek hastens to draw the analogy with the subject who realizes himself as a proletarian revolutionary, as chosen by History to assume this task (p. 18). And the Lacanian notion of 'forced choice' is promptly brought to bear to explain Žižek's position further. But it is clear that the analogy of proletarian and religious commitment is not quite the same as in the earlier work. The former is no longer interpreted merely as resembling the latter, but by means of concepts drawn from the latter.

In all this there is an obvious problem: that this theory of choice leads to an empty voluntarism, which dissolves liberal suspension of judgment, but might as well opt for right-wing as for left-wing positions. The example of Heidegger seems warning enough. But Žižek's more general argument against the liberal equation of socialist and fascist alignments needs to be put in the fuller context of the conception of subjectivity he develops in *The Ticklish Subject* — with the help of St Paul.

St Paul

Already in *For They Know Not What They Do*, St Paul was identified with 'the form [of the Christian religion] which has shown its worth in the tradition which is ours' (p. 29). But the discussion of him in *The Ticklish Subject* has a more specific inspiration in the work of Alain Badiou.[13] We have seen already that Žižek insists on the universality of the affirmation of value. For Badiou, St Paul is important because he created the possibility of universal affirmation: a possibility to be asserted against what Badiou identifies as the dominant cultural tendencies: towards cultural and historical relativism on the one hand, and towards a conception of human groups as bearers of an identity defined in terms of victimhood on the other.[14] For Badiou, St Paul is important as the founder of the historical possibility of a universal message. This universality depends on the Pauline connexion between the notions of subject and of law: a subject without identity and a law without support (p. 6).

For Badiou, the subject emerges in the wake of an Event that breaks the existing order of Being in the sense that it cannot be accounted for by the situation it disturbs.[15] The Event is the emergence of Truth: thus the French Revolution reveals the Truth of the *ancien régime*, the excesses and inconsistencies it lived on and covered up. The subject comes after the Event, and is defined by his or her fidelity to the event, by the persistent discernment of its traces in his or her own situation (*TS*, 130–1). Revealingly, Žižek cites both the Christian religion ('which perhaps provides *the* example of a Truth-event,' Christ's incarnation and death (p. 130)) and the October Revolution, a 'more appropriate' instance to cite today against 'opportunistic leftist "fools" and conservative "knaves"' (p. 131). Žižek's own example here brings out the link between fidelity and subjecthood.

There are traces here, as Žižek suggests, of the Althusserian concept of ideological interpellation. There is a difference, certainly, in their epistemologies: 'Badiou's opposition of knowledge and truth seems to turn exactly around Althusser's opposition of ideology and science' (p. 145). But perhaps more important is the difference between their points of departure, between the basic problems the respective theories address: Althusser is concerned with ideology as that which reproduces the relations of production, Badiou with truth as that which escapes reproduction, and affirms change. Althusser's theory of ideology may explain why subjects act as they do, but does not directly address the universalizing dimension of their action (the extent to which they conceive themselves as acting on and on behalf of others). But for Badiou as for Žižek, the affirmation of Truth, though grounded in concrete circumstances, is necessarily universal. This universality has nothing to do with the neutral apprehension of an objective fact. 'One can discern the signs of an Event in the [objective] Situation only from a previous Decision for Truth, just as in Jansenist theology in which divine miracles are legible as such only in those who have already decided for Faith' (p. 136). The neutral perspective denies the Event, say, the French Revolution, as such, seeing only a multitude of occurrences: the naming makes the Event (pp. 136–37, 141).[16] The reference to Jansenism only enforces the point we have already encountered: we can give reasons for our belief, but the reasons are only valid within the frame of reference of the belief. And here we encounter again the problem encountered earlier does not this make all ideological alignments equivalent? Is there any way to distinguish a true Event and its semblance? The problem seems all the more acute if one accepts, as do Žižek and Badiou, the Christ-event, as reinterpreted by St Paul, as the model of this emergence of subjectivity. For both Badiou and Žižek make it perfectly clear that they do not believe that Jesus rose from the dead.[17] Badiou accepts that the 'truth' proclaimed by St Paul, the resurrection of Jesus, was a mere fable: but when the fabulous content of the message is abandoned, the form, the foundational subjective gesture, remains.[18] (Just as one might argue that Pascal's account of the *formal* mechanisms of ideology is independent of his particular ideological attachment). But Žižek does not find this quite sufficient: 'The problem remains of how it was possible for the first and still most pertinent description of the mode of operation of the fidelity to a Truth-Event to occur apropos of a Truth-Event that is a mere semblance, not an actual Truth' (*TS*, 143). It is not surprising that he cites the case of Heidegger again.

The suggestion he makes is that the paradox whereby the ultimate Truth-Event is a non-event reveals the nature of all fidelity to the Truth-Event: 'What if the true fidelity to the Event is "dogmatic" in the precise sense of unconditional Faith, of an attitude which does not ask for good reasons and which, for that very reason, cannot be refuted by any "argumentation"?' (p. 144).

On the other hand, faith can access reasons that justify it at least to itself. Thus he can show the inadequacy of the Heideggerian analysis of choice as lying in lack of insight into 'the radically *antagonistic* nature of every hitherto communal way of life' (p. 20). The October Revolution was an Event, the Fascist 'Revolution' a pseudo-event, leaving intact the the fundamental level of production relations (p. 200). Marxism draws a dividing-line between subjective positions, not essentialist categories: the Nazis, displacing social antagonisms into racial difference, killed Jews *because they were Jews* (the Stalinist purges rested on the idea that the accused were subjectively committed to counter-revolutionary activity (even if this were a grotesque fiction) (pp. 227–28)). These reasons, though, might not convince the liberal.

Žižek's discussion of choice in terms of grace specifically echoes Badiou. Badiou speaks of extracting a formal and totally secularized conception of grace from the mythological kernel. St Paul had insisted that there can be no pre-conditions, such as prior membership of an existing community, of access to the truth (*Saint Paul*, p. 15). Likewise, a materialism of grace must be founded on the idea that 'toute existence peut un jour être transie par ce qui lui arrive, et se dévouer dès lors à ce qui vaut pour tous' (p. 70) (any human life can be pierced one day by what befalls it, and devote itself thenceforth to what counts for everyone). Badiou retains from orthodox Christian theology the notion that grace is first and foremost gratuitous: it cannot be earned by human efforts.[19] Žižek is at one with Badiou on this point: 'any individual can be "touched by Grace", and interpellated as a proletarian subject' (*TS*, 227). Earlier in *The Ticklish Subject*, under the heading 'Towards a Materialist Theory of Grace,' he discusses the work of the Catholic philosopher Nicolas Malebranche (1638–1715). Malebranche is cited as a further witness to the characteristic modern separation of the act of decision from its content (p. 115). What fascinates Žižek about Malebranche is that his theory of grace is inspired by his occasionalist theory of causality, according to which God, working through general laws, is the only true cause, other so-called causes being simply 'occasions' of the manifestation of the laws. What is left for human freedom is merely consent to the operation of God's laws inside us: 'Is not this reduction of freedom to the "nothing" of an empty gesture the "truth" of the Hegelian Absolute Subject?' (p. 119).[20]

The Christian Legacy

Considering the religious references in *The Ticklish Subject*, one might be surprised by the opening of *The Fragile Absolute*: 'One of the most deplorable aspects of the postmodern era and its so-called "thought" is the return of the religious dimension in all its different guises' (*FA*, 1). But rather than advocating a global evacuation of the religious tradition, Žižek insists that Marxism is in a direct lineage from Christianity and that Marxism should be ready to defend the authentic Christian legacy against both religious fundamentalism and new spiritualisms (p. 2).

What is at stake here can be seen in Žižek's denunciation of New Age-ism, a leitmotif of his recent work. The notion is common currency that our contemporary plight results from *hubris*, an arrogant assumption that we are at the centre of the universe, and entitled to dominate all other beings for our own purposes: this assumption is traced both to the 'Cartesian subject,' and beyond that to the whole Judaeo-Christian tradition. It should be abandoned in favour of a vision of ourselves as necessarily situated within a cosmic order. Now Žižek rejects this theoretically: the excess of subjectivity is the only hope of redemption (*TS*, 132). But the very term 'redemption' emphasizes the fact that his rejection of this doctrine is (also) theological. He is rejecting New Age thought as a neo-paganism. In *The Fragile Absolute* he sets out a model of the pagan Cosmos as a hierarchical order of cosmic principles requiring to be kept in balance: the analogy to this is a vision of society in which to be good is to act in accordance with one's place in the social edifice (p. 119).[21] The idea that an individual has instead an *immediate* access to universality is characteristic of Christianity (though also of Buddhism) (p. 120). Christian love enjoins us to 'unplug' from the organic community into which we were born (p. 121). (In this sense, it is in sympathy with the authentic Hegelianism Žižek has elsewhere defended, which advocates the espousal of 'abstract negativity' against identification with the community into which one is born (*TS*, 94–5, and see above, p. 129.)

In this case, one can see the Christian reference as sharpening our focus on the contemporary predicament, making the stakes of choice more visible. But there are clearly more general problems with this appeal to the Christian legacy. Some of them would apply to all religions: the secular rationalist could simply point to the evils of bigotry, superstition and fanaticism. Žižek's reply, as I take it, would be that the secular tradition tends towards a fiction of impartial rationality that in fact sustains the existing order (*TS*, 223). But there are difficulties more specific to Christianity: its legacy, after all, includes anti-Semitism, even if not all anti-Semitism is Christian in inspiration. Selective appropriation, then, would be the only option, and Žižek's appropriation is selective. But then again, if one's dual frame of reference is Marxism and psychoanalysis, how far is it pertinent to invoke a *Christian* legacy, as distinct from a Judaeo-Christian, or simply Jewish, one? This problem poses itself acutely when Žižek considers a possible psychoanalytic critique of Christianity. Thus, Christianity appears to hold that the fundamental violence underlying every order can be neutralized by confession; psychoanalysis, however, 'far from being a confessionary mode of discourse, entails the acceptance and admission that all our discursive formations are forever haunted by some "indivisible remainder", by some traumatic spectral "rest" that resists "confession", that is, integration into the symbolic universe' (p. 98). In this, it seems to have more in common with Judaism, as presented by Žižek (pp. 97–8). Again, Christianity is often criticized as a religion that generates and that thrives on guilt. Judaism, as Žižek points out, does not, for what matters in it is obedience to the Law, not the inner dispositions of the subject. Christianity, however, with its insistence that you can sin in your heart without any transgressive external action, turns the subject inward in anxious and debilitating self-questioning, installs the rule of a tyrannical superego (pp. 140–3).

For Žižek, the solution to both these problems is the same, and it is provided by the Epistle to the Romans, which is indeed the core of his selective appropriation of the Christian tradition.[22] St Paul is not asserting that the particularity of sin can be integrated into the universal domain of the law, he is calling on us to leave behind the domain of the law itself (p. 100), to 'break out of the vicious superego cycle of the Law and its transgression via Love' (p. 145). What love involves is at one level 'the modest dispensing of spontaneous goodness' (rather than a self-suppressing duty to others) (p. 100); at another it is 'the "concrete" freedom of the loving acceptance of others, of experiencing oneself as free, as finding full realization in relating to others (...) a Yes! to life in its mysterious synchronic multitude' (p. 103). But it can also involve the much more troubling notion of the suspension of the ethical.

This notion has been already discussed in *The Ticklish Subject*. There its content is explicitly political. The liberal centre presents itself as neutrally relying on the role of law. The true leftist response is to insist on the necessity of the suspension of the law (assimilated to the suspension of the ethical). There is a right-wing suspension of the law, but this is intrinsically anti-universal, designed to sustain particular, national or ethnic, interests: whereas the Left 'legitimizes its suspension of the Ethical precisely by means of a reference to the true Universality to come' (p. 223). And this means 'identifying with the symptom': the element (such as the homeless, or illegal immigrants) within the actual social order that challenges its claims to universality: it means asserting universalism from a divisive position. Not a position conferred by some prior belonging, but a subjective stance towards a Truth-Event (pp. 224–7).[23]

In *The Fragile Absolute*, the disquieting elements of this notion are fully emphasized. The properly modern ethical act *is* the act that suspends the ethical: and the illustration Žižek chooses is Sethe in Toni Morrison's *Beloved*, who kills her own daughter lest she be brought back into slavery. 'One bears witness to one's fidelity to the Thing by *sacrificing (also) the Thing itself*' (p. 154: Žižek's emphasis). By the same token, commitment to democracy in Serbia can only be realized on condition that Kosovo is sacrificed (pp. 156–7). But the archetypal figure of this sacrifice is God himself, whose sacrifice of his son gives birth to a 'new subject no longer rooted in a particular substance, redeemed of all particular links (the 'Holy Spirit')' (p. 158). And the Holy Spirit, or Holy Ghost, is identified with 'the community of believers *qua* uncoupled outcasts from the social order — with, ideally, authentic psychoanalytical and revolutionary political collectives as its two main forms' (p. 160).

In *The Ticklish Subject* Žižek imagines a reading of St Paul carried out in the spirit of Lenin's reading of Hegel's *Logic*. It would contain comments like: 'The first part of this sentence provides the deepest insight into Lacanian ethics, while the second part is just theological rubbish!' (p. 149). What the foregoing might suggest is that the commentator would not always have an easy task in distinguishing the two elements: that 'theological rubbish' requires not to be dismissed but re-read for its potential insights into politico-ethical activity. Žižek continues to find in Christian theology a supply both of metaphors and of categories for the understanding of ideology, and he challenges us to ponder the implications of this.[24]

MICHAEL MORIARTY
Queen Mary, University of London

NOTES

1 The following works of Žižek's are discussed here: *The Sublime Object of Ideology* (London, Verso, 1989: hereafter *SOI*); *For They Know Not What They Do: Enjoyment as a Political Factor* (London, Verso, 1991: hereafter *FTKN*); *The Ticklish Subject: the Absent Centre of Political Ontology* (London, Verso, 1999: hereafter *TS*); *The Fragile Absolute: or, Why Is the Christian Legacy Worth Fighting For?* (London, Verso, 2000: hereafter *FA*).

2 Etienne Balibar, *Spinoza et la politique* (Paris, Presses Universitaires de France, 1985); Pierre Macherey, *Hegel ou Spinoza* (Paris, Maspéro, 1979).

3 Louis Althusser, 'Ideology and Ideological State Apparatuses: Notes towards an Investigation,' in *Essays on Ideology* (London, Verso, 1984), pp. 1–60: on Pascal, see p. 42, and cf. Louis Althusser *Sur la philosophie* (Paris, Gallimard, 1994), pp. 52–3. Pascal was a figure of interest to French Marxists in the 1950s, with Henri Lefebvre and Lucien Goldmann both writing substantial books on him.

4 The reference is to the 'wager' fragment: Pascal, *Pensées*, ed. by Louis Lafuma (Paris: Seuil, 1962), fragment 418.

5 *Pensées*, fragment 821, quoted by Žižek, *SOI*, 36. Žižek quotes in the Penguin translation (*Pensées* (Harmondsworth, 1966), p. 274).

6 See, e.g., Jean Mesnard, *Les Pensées de Pascal*, second edition (Paris, SEDES, 1993), pp. 86–87, 174.

7 Pascal, *Pensées*, ed. by Philippe Sellier, Classiques Garnier (Paris, Bordas, 1991), p. 166.

8 Žižek (ed.), *Mapping Ideology* (London, Verso, 1994), 'Introduction,' pp. 12–13.

9 *Pensées*, fragment 60 (Penguin translation, p. 46).

10 The question is, though, whether we can expect these reasons to convince anybody else. The statement that 'the reasons why we should believe are persuasive only to those who already believe' (*SOI*, 38) implies the answer 'no'.

11 Compare the later analysis of the stain or residue of 'enjoyment,' the presence within the subject of the 'obscene call to enjoyment' that is at stake in the submission to totalitarianism (*FTKN*, 231–41). The enjoyment of the renunciation of enjoyment is in fact a constant theme of seventeenth-century Augustinian writing.

12 Here Žižek's gloss is undoubtedly valid: it is borne out not simply by the fragment on custom (see above n. 9) which he quotes at length again here, but by other passages, such as fragment 828.

13 St Paul, as Žižek reminds us (*TS*, 152–3) is also invoked by Lacan; and it would be instructive to compare Žižek's use of religious vocabulary with Lacan's own.

14 Alain Badiou, *Saint Paul: la Fondation de l'universalisme* (Paris: Presses Universitaires de France, 1997), pp. 7, 11–12. Žižek suggests that Badiou can be read 'as the last great author in the French tradition of Catholic dogmatists from Pascal and Malebranche on' (p. 142). It is, though, important to point out that Badiou owes no allegiance to this tradition as such. His own background, he states, is irreligious and anti-clerical (*Saint Paul*, p. 1). This situation is quite unlike, say, Althusser's.

15 Žižek's exposition also draws on Badiou's *L'Être et l'événement* (Paris, Seuil, 1988). It is worth noting that he parts company with Badiou's conception of subjectivity (see *TS*, 153–67): but as to the points discussed here I take them to be in agreement.

16 Compare *FTKN*, pp. 29, 78.

17 'Any location of the Truth-Event at the level of supernatural miracles necessarily entails regression into obscurantism, since the event of Science is irreducible and cannot be undone' (*The Ticklish Subject*, p. 142). A believer might reply that a miracle is precisely that which undoes or transcends the order of nature revealed by science.

18 Badiou, *Saint Paul*, p. 6.

19 This is not solely a Protestant notion. The Roman Catholic tradition accepts the contribution of human effort to the process of salvation, but holds that grace is none the less a gratuitous gift.

20 The point being that there is no Hegelian Absolute Subject, in the sense of a unitary entity encompassing human subjectivity (cf. *TS*, 88–9). But if the Malebranchian model is adopted, one would need to investigate the general laws, the particular laws, and the occasional causes that regulate the flow of grace (that is, put us in possession of our beliefs — that expression to be understood both as an objective and a subjective genitive). The work of Pierre Bourdieu could be read in terms of such a project.

21 He elsewhere rejects the reading of Hegel as endorsing a similar model of society (*TS*, 94).

22 Žižek has stated that 'what I find theoretically and politically engaging in the religious legacy is not the abstract messianic promise of some redemptive Otherness, but, on the contrary, religion in its properly dogmatic and institutional aspect' (*The Žižek Reader*, ed. by Elizabeth Wright and Edmond Wright (Oxford, Blackwell, 1999), Preface, p. ix). But he says little in *The Fragile Absolute* about dogma and institutions.

23 The subjective stance recommended by Žižek involves a reaffirmation of the traditional Marxist thesis of the primacy of the economy (pp. 225–6, 356).

24 Derrida observes that for Marx religion is not one ideology among others: it holds a privileged place in the analysis of ideology in general (*Les Spectres de Marx: l'Etat de la dette, le travail du deuil et la nouvelle Internationale* (Paris, Galilée, 1993), p. 236).

As If: Traversing the Fantasy in Žižek

One of the distinguishing features of Žižek's work is its capacity to be both predictable and original at the same time. It reads into culture and philosophy the same Lacanian structures, drawing the same conclusions. Yet it is precisely this overdetermination that allows him to see his examples as no one else has. Reading his books has been compared to using a CD ROM — 'click here, go there, use this fragment, that story or scene[1] — an analogy which suggests that despite the enormous wealth of material Žižek explores throughout his work, the explorations are conducted in the name of an overall project which remains consistent in its theoretical basis and aims. There is also a standard interpretative procedure in his work: typically Žižek will introduce an object of attention (a philosophical idea, a social event, a film), tell us how it is usually interpreted, then bring it all into focus with an expert adjustment of the lens until suddenly we are 'looking awry' at the object. Then he explains that in fact this is nothing other than a precise exemplification of this or that process in Lacan.

Take his reading of *The Silence of the Lambs*, for example.[2] The film was a success worldwide owing to its shocking depiction of the serial killer Hannibal (the 'Cannibal') Lecter, a supremely intelligent former psychiatrist who is also capable of extreme depravity, eating the flesh of those he murders. But for Žižek the horrific events depicted in the film are there only as a pretext for what lies at its core, which is nothing other than an accurate portrayal of a Lacanian analytic session. Starling comes to Lecter so that he might help her catch another serial killer currently on the loose, Buffalo Bill, who has just abducted another victim. Lecter agrees to help, on one condition — that she tell him about herself. Immediately she is reconstituted as psychoanalytic patient, Lecter her therapist. He swiftly gets her to speak of the key event in her personal history, when her father's murder made her an orphan at the age of 10. In the next short session (he is a Lacanian analyst, after all) he extracts from her a primal scene as beautifully nightmarish and resonant as any in Freud. Forced to live with relatives on a sheep and horse ranch, the newly orphaned Clarice wakes up one night hearing a terrifying noise: the screaming of lambs as they are slaughtered. She rescues one and runs away, only to be caught soon after, her lamb killed with the rest. Lecter's diagnosis is devastating:

'You still wake up sometimes, don't you? You hear the screaming of the lambs, and you think that if you could save poor Catherine [Buffalo Bill's victim] you could make them stop, don't you? You think if Catherine lives, you won't wake up in the dark ever again, to that awful screaming of the lambs'. Clarice murmurs, unconvincingly, that she doesn't know. Lecter does. His diagnosis has propelled him to a state of epistemophilic bliss: 'Thank you, Clarice. Thank you'.

Our fascination with Lecter, Žižek argues, lies in his combination of unimaginable horror and boundless reason. As such he is the product of our simultaneous deep longing for a Lacanian analyst and inability to apprehend the powerful way Lacanian analysis will tear into our flimsy sense of individuality. Lecter's real cannibalism is his devouring of the very stuff of Clarice's being. Her primal scene is the 'fundamental fantasy,' that which holds subjectivity together, covering up the real; her desire to stop the lambs from crying supports her symbolic identity, determining the course of her life, driving her on in her ambition to transcend her humble origins and become an FBI agent. Lecter's exposure of this fact, says Žižek, is in keeping with the ultimate function of Lacanian analysis: to enable the subject to 'traverse the fantasy' by disclosing the *objet a*, revealing what is in the subject more than the subject. There is one crucial difference, though: Lecter is not cruel enough to be a Lacanian analyst. He helps her track down Buffalo Bill, but 'in psychoanalysis, we must pay the analyst so that he or she will allow us to offer him or her our *Dasein* on a plate' (Žižek, 1994, 53).

This brilliant reading reminds us that Žižek's project amounts to a strikingly original exercise in cultural studies. It conforms to the standard psychoanalytic approach to cultural analysis, in that it suggests how unconscious processes challenge and motivate the surface meanings of culture. Yet where cultural studies tends to use the insights of theory to support its readings of contemporary culture (much more reductively than Žižek in fact), Žižek audaciously turns this relationship around, so that philosophy, psychoanalysis and political theory are interrogated by examples from art and culture. *Richard II* 'proves beyond any doubt that Shakespeare had read Lacan' (Žižek, 1991a, 9), everything you always wanted to know about Lacan can be asked of Hitchcock, and the inversion of Kant's categorical imperative is anticipated by the makers of German fat-free salami (Žižek, 1999a, 5).[3] More importantly, though, behind his analysis of the film lies what is Žižek's fundamental aim: to present an accurate version of the complex constitution of the (post) modern subject.

The point of departure for his project is his conviction that we are witnessing, in postmodernity, a shift in the notion of subjectivity. This is most visible in cinema, which he has described as his equivalent of Freud's 'royal road' to the unconscious, for in 'ordinary commercial films [like *The Silence of the Lambs*] ... you can detect what goes on at the profoundest, most radical level of our symbolic identities and how we experience ourselves' (Lovink, 1995). But it is also central to postmodernist and poststructuralist theory (representatives of which, for Žižek, are Derrida, Butler, Deleuze and Foucault, among others). Postmodern practice and theory both assume a decline in the function of a monolithic paternal authority which dictates fixed subject positions and social practices. The result is that subjectivity is now envisaged as a liberating process of 'performativity,' of continually reshaping and choosing alternative subject positions.[4] For Žižek this is too simplistic theoretically, for it fails to recognize — unlike Lacan, or the German Idealists whom he sees as anticipating Lacan — the extent to which the subject is formed and continues to be motivated by a powerful extradiscursive force, which he calls 'the truly traumatic core of the modern subject'.[5] The perceived decline of the big Other figures, in other words, as postmodern theory's 'fundamental fantasy'. Throughout his work Žižek effectively plays Hannibal Lecter to postmodernism's Clarice Starling, taking it 'through the fantasy' by reminding it that its version of the liberated subject is an illusion — one which, moreover, effectively plays into the hands of global capitalism and its rhetoric about our freedom to choose different identities and ways of life through consumption. Žižek aims to achieve this by countering the fantasmatic postmodern conception of the subject with a properly Lacanian version, married to a Marxist critique of political economy. Ultimately, his willingness to blend Marxism with Lacan means that Žižek is as generous as Hannibal Lecter, too, offering in return for exposing the postmodern fantasy of subjectivity an idea of how his alternative Lacanian version of the subject might service a Marxist commitment to emancipation.

At the end of the 1950s Lacan began to move away from the relation between the symbolic and the imaginary in favour of a sustained interrogation of the interplay between the symbolic and the real.[6] This Lacan is Žižek's Lacan — the 'real' Lacan, we might say-and he expounds his ideas faithfully and imaginatively. But Žižek's own individual slant means that there are subtle but telling shifts of emphasis in his reading.[7] His starting-point is the powerful narrative of loss and trauma that is the Lacanian account of subjectivization. The child passes from a period of satisfying, nourishing bodily contact with the mother's body, experienced as a state of excess and plenitude, to a position as speaking subject in the symbolic order. Žižek's understanding of the symbolic order is true to its Lacanian (which is to say its Saussurean) sense as the arbitrary system of meanings into which we divide our world, an entity which pre-exists us, and into which we are born, learning and abiding by its rules. The symbolic is, in short, our 'everyday reality' or culture. More than Lacan, though, Žižek emphasizes how it *feels* to live within this conceptual framework. The symbolic figures in his work (not surprisingly, perhaps, given his experiences of totalitarianism in Yugoslavia) as a kind of faceless bureaucratic system made up of inexplicable rules and regulations which we have no option but to follow.[8] Its anonymity and vaguely sinister air is conveyed by its alternative name, 'the big Other'. One of Žižek's favourite points of reference is Kafka, and his work similarly conveys the sheer absurdity of our relationship with the symbolic order. It reminds us that the symbolic gets its name because it is made up of things which stand in for real things. It is an arbitrary, contingent network built on thin air, but which nevertheless regulates our desires and provides us with our destiny, our history, our very sense of reality. Everyday reality, in other words, is always *ideological*-subjects are forever trapped in the process of interpellation, coaxed by the various apparatuses of the state into taking their places in the social order (and if they won't be coaxed, the apparatus forces them). Althusser's theory was heavily influenced by Lacan's conception of the imaginary, the realm in which we falsely experience ourselves as whole beings through misrecognising ourselves in external images and in others. We misrecognise ourselves in ideology so that we believe our subject position is natural or perfectly suited to who we take ourselves to be. And like both theorists Žižek holds that our symbolic identity is supported and sustained by the imaginary (though he prefers to focus on just one imaginary mechanism, fantasy). Being a subject is an absurd, though quite necessary, experience of being held in place by two kinds of illusory force: the big Other and the distorting, falsifying framework of the imaginary.

Set against the everyday world made up of symbolic and imaginary, however, is 'another world,' or at least another kind of thing altogether, the *real*, that which is unsymbolized and unsymbolizable. We can think of the Lacanian real by pointing to its operation in two main spheres, the 'physical' and the 'psychic,' which are not separate but two different aspects of the same phenomenon (not unlike Spinoza's two modes of substance, 'Extension' and 'Thought'). To begin with, the real functions in the external world, as it were. The symbolic order is drawn from Saussure's idea of the way sign-systems divide up the world into distinct entities. Physical experience is always mediated through a conceptual framework: we have direct access to the phenomenal world through our bodies (we come into physical contact with the objects that surround us) but can only make sense of things through language. In its simplest sense Lacan's real is the material world we are cut off from after entering the symbolic, but which is all the time *there*, 'beneath' the symbolic. In a more complex and more crucial sense, the real also signifies the bodily drives which are regulated by the symbolic. The second sphere in which the real functions is internal psychic space. This incorporates the pre-imaginary period of blissful plenitude in the relationship with the mother — an aspect of the real which is continually *referred* to by the imaginary and by desire, but which can be reproduced by neither. This real also includes the experience of trauma, which also refers to the pre-imaginary state by returning us to the helpless, speechless state of earliest childhood, and to death, the final triumph of the real which puts an end to meaning and the subject.

Both uses of the real are relevant to Žižek. But most important to him are the implications of each sense of the term. More than simply that which is 'covered' by the symbolic, the real is the *opposite* of the symbolic order, precisely how 'reality' would 'look' had the symbolic not been imposed upon it — that is, a mass of matter all merged into one total block, not divided up by signs, like the 'grey and formless mist, pulsing slowly as if with inchoate life' outside the car window in Robert Heinlein's sci-fi novel *The Unpleasant Profession of Jonathan Hoag* (Žižek, 1991a, 14). This reminds us why the real gets *its* name. It is the opposite of the symbolic world of appearance, how things 'really' are, before the imposition of an artificial network of arbitrary signs. This is something that the subject has an instinctive awareness of. We sense that the symbolic is artificial and we sense that the real is constantly there, ready to stretch the logic of the symbolic to breaking-point or puncture its flimsy structure. Even though the symbolic is a sham, this is not necessarily cause to rejoice, for we cannot pursue an authentic independent identity without it. Nevertheless our apprehension of an anarchic other place where meaning breaks down is the powerful motivating force beyond all others in our lives. It is also the key to popular culture, which draws its energies from the same tension.

At the heart of Žižek's work, then, is the idea that both our identity and culture are failed attempts to organize an essentially archaic core into a system. Both are founded upon and motivated by a central void, or lack. It is this element which Žižek believes is central to the philosophical tradition that begins with Descartes and continues through the work of German Idealism from Kant to Hegel, where subjectivity is founded upon an element of excess — Hegel's 'Night of the World' — which is then immediately 'renormalized'. The symbolic order gives an individual identity by providing him or her with a subject position, a linguistic 'point of reference'. But it never accounts for who we *really* are. The symbolic coordinates which give us our social identity can only circulate around, never represent, the lack at the centre. It is this which Žižek calls the 'truly traumatic core of the modern subject' (Žižek, 1999b, xi) and which is overlooked, he thinks, by the poststructuralist or postmodernist conviction that the subject is always merely the *effect* of language, power, desire, ideology, whatever. Similarly the cultural world which we inhabit is a symbolic frame which only *roughly* equates to the real, in the way that a map relates to geographical reality without quite covering it. And the crucial point for Žižek is that the void at the heart of the subject is correlative to the void at the heart of the symbolic. The link is manifested principally in moments of *jouissance*, the Lacanian term Žižek translates as 'enjoyment' (thereby investing the term with more of a connotation of power). Enjoyment is a kind of excessive pleasure — so excessive in fact that, paradoxically, it becomes painful-which transgresses the prohibitions of the symbolic. It features in several different ways in the life of the subject: through the neurotic symptom, which the subject 'enjoys' because it provides a certain satisfaction (as well as suffering), in the unsymbolizable moment of sexual orgasm, a physical space beyond language, and in the ultimate enjoyment forbidden by the Oedipus complex, incest with the mother. Žižek's use of the term is more general, referring to those moments when intense pleasure is taken in the collapse of the symbolic, those points when meaning breaks down. He often describes this with a pun: 'enjoy-*meant*'.

Enjoyment is crucial to understanding the symbiotic relationship between the subject and culture. Because both are motivated by the 'hard kernel of the real' (one of Žižek's favourite phrases, perhaps because it recalls Lenin's description of the 'rational kernel' of Hegelian dialectic) at their core, the subject seeks out aspects of his world which expose the gaps in the otherwise 'closed system' of the symbolic order. More specifically this involves taking particular objects and investing them with a personalized libidinal energy. In the 'eyes' of the symbolic, 'stupid' and sclerotic, all objects are of equal value, in the Saussurean sense of language having 'no positive terms'. Yet our quest for enjoyment means that we refuse to see some things — and what these are varies from subject to subject — as equal to others. They become elements of the real, evidence of the void in both the subject and culture. Žižek calls the object which we invest with private enjoyment in this way *objet petit a*, Lacan's term for the way our unconscious bestows on particular objects, other people, certain kinds of voice and gaze, the psychic significance of the ultimate lost object (lost, that is, in the real), the mother's body. As an example Žižek uses Patricia Highsmith's story, 'The Black House,' in which an old dilapidated house unaccountably becomes the source of the fears of a group of people in the town. This, he suggests, demonstrates how 'a quite ordinary, everyday object . . . starts to function as a kind of screen, an empty space on which the subject projects the fantasies that support his desire, a surplus of the real that propels us to narrate again and again our first traumatic encounters with *jouissance*' (Žižek, 1991a, 133).

This reading of *objet a*, the object which motivates our desire and which cannot be accounted for by the symbolic, explains the title of Žižek's *The Sublime Object of Ideology*.[9] Published in 1989 this book was Žižek's breakthrough work, his first to reach a wide European and Anglo-American readership. His intervention in the theory of ideology is, arguably, the aspect of his work which remains the most influential across the widest range of academic disciplines. Ideology was famously defined by Althusser as 'the imaginary ways we represent to ourselves our real conditions of existence'.[10] While Žižek's apprehension of the illusory nature of everyday reality is strongly reminiscent of Althusser he differs by insisting that the illusions of the cultural world are motivated by what it cannot represent or account for, the real. Another way of putting this is to say that Žižek's work on ideology shows that Althusser's definition of ideology depends on only two of Lacan's three orders of existence: those *imaginary* ways we relate to *symbolic* reality. What of the *real*? Without it, Althusser never moves beyond two forms of illusory construction-the imaginary and the symbolic. Žižek's revision of Althusser (though he never puts it like this) might read: 'Ideology is the imaginary ways we represent to ourselves our symbolic conditions of existence thereby covering up the disturbing nature of the real'.

For Žižek ideology is nothing less than the way we cope with the truth that subjectivity and social reality are each constructed around a traumatic void. Ideology is thus much more complex than Marxist critique has hitherto realized. When we take into account the real, Žižek says, 'it is no longer sufficient to denounce the "artificial" character of the ideological experience, to demonstrate the way the object experienced by ideology as "natural" and "given" is effectively a discursive construction, a result of a network of symbolic overdetermination' (Žižek, 1991a, 129). Žižek thus complicates two key tenets of ideology critique, the notion that ideology is a particular kind of discourse, and the idea that there is an alternative 'reality' behind the false one maintained by ideology. Ideology does preserve a false version of reality, but behind it is the *real*, a realm beyond signification, not another symbolic order. The key to Žižek's argument is the Lacanian conception of *fantasy*, defined by Lacan as the relation of the barred subject to the *objet a* ($\$◇a$). The function of fantasy is to fill the void created by the real. It creates a space, a kind of blank screen on which the subject's desires can be projected. In this way, fantasy *realizes* desire-not in the sense of satisfying it, but by bringing it out in the open, giving it a shape. And this is precisely what ideology does. One of the most striking aspects of Žižek's theory of ideology is his insistence that, though it might seem otherwise, fantasy serves to support ideology rather than challenge it. It is natural to think of fantasy as an escape into a realm of wish-fulfilment, divorced from reality, but Žižek emphasizes that reality actually *depends* upon subscribing to the fantasy. This accounts for another revision of Althusser's theory. Many readers of his work have pointed out that Althusser does not satisfactorily explain *why* the subject is so willing to be interpellated. Žižek suggests that it is because there is something fundamentally attractive about ideology which goes beyond its content. We sense the symbolic order is a purely bureaucratic mechanism designed to keep us in our subject positions. We also intuitively apprehend the real is beneath it all the while. Fantasy is what enables us to cover up this knowledge and continue to function as normal subjects, to continue to make life 'meaningful' in the symbolic.

Žižek demonstrates that there is a characteristic *doubleness* about ideology. The ideological fantasy manages to cover up the real and persuade us to accept the logic of the symbolic, but by doing so draws attention to the fact that the real is what the symbolic order is built upon and is continually ready to shatter it. One of his best examples concerns the familiar safety rituals we are taken through on aeroplanes as they take off. He asks:

Aren't they sustained by a fantasmatic scenario of how a possible plane-crash will look? After a gentle landing on water (miraculously, it is always supposed to happen on water!), each of the passengers puts on the life-jacket and, as on a beach toboggan, slides into the water and takes a swim, like a nice collective lagoon holiday experience under the guidance of an experienced swimming instructor.[11]

In this scenario, the fantasy enables us to imagine that we will be safe in the event of a plane crash, even though we know perfectly well this is unlikely to be the case. Thus, the fantasy simultaneously covers up the real and draws attention to it. It expresses the very thing, the horrible reality of a plane crash, which has been repressed, which cannot otherwise be symbolized. The mechanism works on a more explicitly political level, too. In *Looking Awry* Žižek gives a reading of two films which portray persecutory totalitarian worlds, Terry Gilliams's *Brazil* and Rainer Fassbinder's *Lili Marleen*. Each film is named after the popular song which resounds throughout, and which functions in two contradictory ways: as a support for the prevailing totalitarian order, a kind of signature-tune for the dominant ideology, making it all seem unified and attractive, but also as a 'fragment of the signifier permeated with idiotic enjoyment'. Each song is 'on the verge of transforming itself into a subversive element that could burst from the very ideological machine by which it is supported' (Žižek, 1991a, 129). *Brazil* ends with the apparent defeat of its hero, who has been broken by savage torture, only for him to escape his oppressors by whistling 'Brazil'.

  Žižek's theory of the ideological fantasy suggests how complex and powerful our relationship with ideology is. Ideology isn't something that cleverly tricks us, making us believe in something we don't. Rather it is effective precisely because it acknowledges what it cannot explain, and because it appeals to precisely the same sense of 'enjoy-*meant*' which threatens to blow it apart. Generally speaking, the theory of ideology before Žižek suggested that we conformed because we didn't know what we were *really* doing. Žižek — influenced here by the work of the German philosopher Peter Sloterdijk[12] — argues that ideology is more a matter of knowing what we do is false but still doing it anyway, just as we know that the lagoon scenario acted out by stewardesses is unlikely to save us in a plane crash but still go along with it. Ideology is something that itself yields enjoyment: we adhere to the Law because it appeals to our enjoyment. This is also why Žižek thinks any theory of contemporary politics or society needs to take account of 'enjoyment as a political factor'. In a number of books (*For They Know Not What They Do*, *The Metastases of Enjoyment* and *The Sublime Object of Ideology*) Žižek explores the role played by enjoyment and the fantasy in oppressive elements of our culture, like totalitarian régimes and racist and homophobic groups. Such communities are held together, he suggests, by the fact that the Law promises a kind of enjoyment as much as it prohibits it. This relationship is secured through the fantasies they share (about, say, the figure of the Jew) which serve both sides of the Law: order and transgression. Žižek's writings on culture and ideology demonstrate how late capitalism — always supported by its 'familiar,' 'liberal democracy'-sustains its dominant position by ensuring that the subject colludes in his/her own subjugation. The idea of knowing what we're doing but still doing it anyway can explain what Sloterdijk calls the 'cynical reasoning' evident in postmodern culture. Nowadays, we all know that presidents lie, yet we still support them. We know that advertisers exaggerate the value of their products, yet we still buy them. More than previous forms, postmodern ideology continually flaunts its own ideological operations: post-ironic advertising draws attention to the whole sham of advertising and its own hyperbole, TV generates endless programs based on the out-take, or what goes on behind the scenes.[13]

All this suggests why it is problematic to equate this knowingness with liberation. In 'You May!,' an article recently published in the *London Review of Books* (particularly interesting because it is a more deliberately accessible statement of the aims of his project), Žižek surveys what he sees as evidence of the dominant attitude of 'reflexiveness' in the postmodern permissive society. In the apparent absence of the symbolic order to instruct us in our social behaviour, 'all our impulses, from sexual orientation to ethnic belonging, are more and more experienced as matters of choice' (Žižek, 1999a, 1): one can choose how to be seduced, how to rewrite one's psychological history, how to be racist. Even psychoanalytic symptoms have 'lost their innocence,' and are shaped according to the subject's knowledge of psychoanalytic theory (Žižek, 1999a, 2). This means that the law no longer operates via repression and the imposition of a strict social hierarchy, but effectively sponsors our acts of transgression, demanding that we 'Enjoy!'. Žižek's argument is to emphasize, firstly, that although on the face of it something has changed in the nature of our relation to the big Other, beneath the surface things are still the same. The apparent endorsement of our transgressive acts by the Other only creates new guilts and anxieties: 'Our postmodern reflexive society which seems hedonistic and permissive is actually saturated with rules and regulations which are intended to serve our well-being (restrictions on smoking and eating, rules against sexual harassment)' (Žižek, 1999a, 5). With the demise of one kind of adherence to the law comes another in its place. The second aspect of his argument is to wonder: if the law regulates our enjoyment, where is the potential for subversion?

The value of the Cartesian and Idealist subject is that it is, in Lacanian terms, properly *hysterical*. The outcome of the Lacanian narrative of subjectivization is that the subject is 'hystericized' by the process: aware that he or she is being compelled to act in a certain way because of the desire of an inscrutable Other. Entering the symbolic order is a matter of being conscripted to a continual process of questioning: what does the Other want me to be? How can I satisfy the desire of the Other? This accounts for what Lacan calls the 'existential value' of the neurotic, its repeated staging of questions that have no answer in the symbolic.[14] In particular, the hysteric throws the Other's question (the *Che vuoi?*) back at it: *why* am I what you say I am? Hysterical discourse testifies to the surplus of the process of symbolization, motivated by that within the subject which cannot be symbolized and is therefore disturbingly 'left over,' becoming a spectral presence haunting intersubjective relations in the symbolic, thus highlighting the ill-fitting nature of the link between symbolic and real (Žižek, 1991a, 131). By contrast the postmodern conception of subjectivity has the structure of 'perversion,' where the subject is aware of precisely what the Other wants and readily turns itself into the required object of desire, offering itself up for the enjoyment of the Other. Perversion means that *jouissance* is derived from identification with the law rather than challenging the law. Thus Žižek gives a standard Marxist form of social analysis a pathological twist (a move which is reminiscent of the Frankfurt School, in particular the notion of 'repressive desublimation'): 'containment' is reformulated as perversion, 'subversion' is equivalent to hysteria. Žižek has often described hysteria in Marxist terms, pointing out that 'hysteria/history is more than a trivial word game — hysteria is the subject's way of resisting the prevailing, historically specified form of interpellation or symbolic indentification'.[15]

Žižek affirms, in other words, that hysteria is both 'normal' and valuable. Here we return to the question of his repetitiveness. The hysterical nature of subjectivity is something which is implied more often than it is stated in Žižek, as time and again he highlights the same process at work in culture and philosophy which exemplifies the failure of the symbolic to account adequately for the subject and its implications. His discussion of *The Silence of the Lambs*, for example, is followed by a demonstration that Magritte's paintings are all variations on the same process — moments when the disturbing nothingness of the real intrudes into the otherwise stable symbolic universe: 'reality is never given in its totality; there is always a void gaping in its midst, filled out by monstrous apparitions' (Žižek, 1994, 57). He concludes: 'It would be possible for us to continue ad infinitum with the variations generated by [this] elementary matrix' (Žižek, 1994, 57). No reader familiar with Žižek's work would doubt this statement for a minute. For the exposure of the 'elementary matrix' upon which all culture and thought is founded is the interpretative strategy at the very core of Žižek's work. But the procedure is in fact so ubiquitous that it seems to exceed the uses to which it is put, taking its place in the foreground where the object of study should be, just as when we notice the extraordinary death's head in *The Ambassadors* (which proves beyond doubt, of course, that Holbein read *The Four Fundamental Concepts of Psychoanalysis*) we cannot look at it in the same way again. The result is that Žižek's interpretative methodology has a rhetoric all of its own. Its value is that it powerfully defamiliarizes our sense of social reality, suggesting that there is something fundamentally absurd and static about our position in society. But it also implies that culture is doomed to repeat the same processes endlessly, because it is founded upon a structure which is transcendent and unalterable. And this has serious implications for Žižek's Marxist critique of political economy, which by definition argues for change.

Žižek occupies a rather paradoxical position for a Marxist. His aim to 're-hystericize' the subject, to return it to its questioning function, has an obvious correlation with his stated commitment to emancipation (in his prefaces to *The Žižek Reader* and *The Ticklish Subject*). But where Marxist 'ideology critique' is, as a rule, geared towards demystifying ideology in order to achieve some kind of greater awareness which can contribute to social change, so deeply rooted in the psychic structure is Žižek's idea of the fantasy that there can be no change: we cannot deal in any other way with the void at the heart of ourselves. Ideology, in other words, is not just inevitable, but *valuable*, because without it we would lapse into neurosis or even psychosis. The implication of his analysis of contemporary culture is that exposing the fantasies which glue our being together might enable us to traverse them. But this is problematic, and not only because it brings us up against the familiar difficulty with psychoanalytic attempts to transpose the personal onto the collective — who would be the equivalent of the analyst? Žižek's notion of the ideological fantasy does not suggest it is a pathological symptom in the psyche of the subject: it is perfectly normal. Time and again he explains how our experience of social reality depends upon 'a certain *as if*': 'we act *as if* we believe in the almightiness of bureaucracy, *as if* the President incarnates the Will of the People, *as if* the Party expresses the objective interest of the working class'. But he also reminds us that if we *do not* act in this way 'the very texture of the social field disintegrates' (Žižek, 1989, 36) — and this is an outcome of a quite different order to political revolution.

Perhaps there is a note of anxiety in all the compulsive energy of Žižek's project: he brilliantly unmasks the workings of ideology *as if* we can overthrow them, but is only too aware that this is impossible. Alternatively, this might well be the source of a certain critical *jouissance* we can detect in his continual affirmation of the unassailable quality of the big Other. In this respect Žižek himself shifts between the hysterical and the perverse positions in his theory: exposing the fragile status of the big Other by questioning it, while also investing in its ultimate status as the Law. Žižek's very method of exposing the ideological mechanism, in other words, reinforces its inevitability. The paradox bears a strong similarity to Baudrillard's critique of Marxism in *The Mirror of Production*, that it depends upon precisely the same ideology (the idea of self-production) as the late-capitalist political economy it claims to deconstruct.[16] Žižek's ubiquitous interpretative mechanism functions as the mirror of the transcendent processes he identifies at the heart of culture. We might even see its status in Žižek's work as the equivalent of the fundamental fantasy at the core of the individual, supporting his very identity as a theorist. Like Clarice Starling, who thinks she need only rescue one more victim and the lambs will stop crying, it is as if Žižek imagines he need give us just one more example of the traumatic encounter with the real and the dominance of the Big Other will be exposed and overthrown.[17] This, as Hannibal Lecter might say, is no more than a fantasy.

BRAN NICOL
University College, Chichester

Works Cited

Louis Althusser (1984) 'Ideology and Ideological State Apparatuses (Notes towards an Investigation)', in *Essays on Ideology* (London: Verso), 1–60.

Jean Baudrillard (1975) *The Mirror of Production*, trans. by Mark Poster (St. Louis: Telos Press).

Peter Dews (1995) 'The Tremor of Reflection: Slavoj Žižek's Lacanian Dialectics', *Radical Philosophy* 72 (July / August 1995), 17–29.

Jacques Lacan (1993), Seminar III, *The Psychoses*, trans. by Russell Grigg (London: Routledge).

Geert Lovink (1995), internet interview with Slavoj Žižek: *http://www.ctheory.com/a37-society_fan.html*.

Peter Osborne (1996) (ed.), 'Lacan in Slovenia: Slavoj Žižek and Renata Salecl', in *A Critical Sense: Interviews with Intellectuals* (London and New York: Routledge), 21–35 (24).

Peter Sloterdijk (1988) *Critique of Cynical Reason* (London and New York: Verso).

Slavoj Žižek (1989) *The Sublime Object of Ideology* (London and New York: Verso).

Slavoj Žižek (1991a) *Looking Awry: an Introduction to Jacques Lacan through Popular Culture* (London: MIT Press).

Slavoj Žižek (1991b) *For They Know Not What They Do* (London and New York: Verso).

Slavoj Žižek (1992) (ed.) *Everything You Always Wanted to Know about Lacan (but were Afraid to Ask Hitchcock* (London and New York: Verso, 1992).

Slavoj Žižek (1993) *Tarrying With the Negative: Kant, Hegel, and the Critique of Ideology* (Durham, NC: Duke University Press).

Slavoj Žižek (1994) 'A Hair of the Dog That Bit You', in Mark Bracher et al, *Lacanian Theory of Discourse: Subject, Structure and Society* (New York and London: New York University Press), 46–73.

Slavoj Žižek (1999a) 'You May!', *London Review of Books,* 21:6 (18th March 1999): *http://www.lrb.co.uk/v21/n06/zize2106.htm*, 1–6.

Slavoj Žižek (1999b) 'Preface: Burning the Bridges', in *The Žižek Reader* (Oxford: Blackwell), ed. by Elizabeth Wright, and Edmond Wright, vii–x.

Slavoj Žižek (1999c) 'Fantasy as a Political Category: A Lacanian Approach', in Elizabeth Wright and Edmond Wright (eds.) *The Žižek Reader* (Oxford: Blackwell), 89–101.

NOTES

* Thanks are due to Ben Noys for his valuable comments and suggestions during the writing of this article.

1 Internet interview with Geert Lovink, 1995: *http://www.ctheory.com/a37-society_fan.html*.

2 Slavoj Žižek, 'A Hair of the Dog That Bit You,' Mark Bracher et al, *Lacanian Theory of Discourse: Subject, Structure and Society* (New York and London: New York University Press, 1994), 46–73.

3 Slavoj Žižek, *Looking Awry: an Introduction to Jacques Lacan through Popular Culture* (London: MIT Press, 1991); Žižek, ed., *Everything You Always Wanted to Know about Lacan (but were Afraid to Ask Hitchcock* (London and New York: Verso, 1992); Žižek, 'You May!,' *London Review of Books*, (vol.21, no.6, 18th March 1999), *http://www.lrb.co.uk/v21/n06/zize2106.htm*, 1–6.

4 It should be pointed out that Žižek's generalizations about poststructuralism and postmodernism are at least as problematic as the oversimplified versions of subjectivity he accuses this diverse group of theorists as advancing, except perhaps in the cases of Judith Butler or Laclau and Mouffe.

5 Slavoj Žižek, 'Preface: Burning the Bridges,' *The Žižek Reader* (Oxford: Blackwell, 1999), ed. by Elizabeth Wright, and Edmond Wright, vii-x.

6 The break is visible in Seminar VII, *The Ethics of Psychoanalysis*.

7 It is important to bear in mind the difference in intellectual context between Žižek's work and that of his master. We could identify (following Lenin's reading of Marx's three sources) three main elements in Žižek's philosophical constitution: a certain 'Frenchness' (his faith in Cartesianism, and the Lacanian/Althusserian lens through which he analyzes society, politics and philosophy) is blended with the German (the Frankfurt School, Freud and Marx) and the 'Slovenian' (a keen surrealist eye for the absurdities of contemporary existence). This is backed up by his experience of being an intellectual in the former Yugoslavia and during its subsequent violent break-up, a background which lends a passion and authority to Žižek's otherwise playful and arcane discourse.

8 In an interview with *Radical Philosophy* in 1990, Žižek described the Yugoslavian régime in similar terms, as an 'extreme form of alientation, a totally non-transparent system that nobody, including those in the power structure, could comprehend'. He suggests that this helps explain the resonance of Lacanian thought in Slovenia in the 1980s. 'Lacan in Slovenia: Slavoj Žižek and Renata Salecl,' in Peter Osborne, ed., *A Critical Sense: Interviews with Intellectuals* (London and New York: Routledge, 1996), 21–35 (24).

9 Slavoj Žižek, *The Sublime Object of Ideology* (London and New York: Verso, 1989).

10 Louis Althusser, 'Ideology and Ideological State Apparatuses (Notes towards an Investigation),' in *Essays on Ideology* (London: Verso, 1984), 1–60.

11 Slavoj Žižek, 'Fantasy as a Political Category: A Lacanian Approach,' in Elizabeth Wright and Edmond Wright (eds.) *The Žižek Reader* (Oxford: Blackwell, 1999), 89–101 (91).

12 Peter Sloterdijk, *Critique of Cynical Reason* (London and New York: Verso, 1988).

13 See Slavoj Žižek, *Tarrying With the Negative: Kant, Hegel, and the Critique of Ideology* (Durham, NC: Duke University Press, 1993).

14 Jacques Lacan, Seminar III, *The Psychoses*, trans. by Russell Grigg (London: Routledge, 1993), 190.

15 Slavoj Žižek, *For They Know Not What They Do* (London and New York: Verso, 1991), 101.

16 Jean Baudrillard, *The Mirror of Production*, trans. by Mark Poster (St. Louis: Telos Press, 1975). There are of course certain interesting similarities between Žižek and Baudrillard, beyond their cult status in contemporary theory. Both are perhaps the most prominent theorists of the object in postmodernism whose work depends upon a central reversal: reality is fundamentally unreal.

17 Other readers have detected a sense of unreality about Žižek's claim that we may come to experience 'the collapse of the big Other' (Žižek, 1993, 237): e.g. Peter Dews in 'The Tremor of Reflection: Slavoj Žižek's Lacanian Dialectics,' *Radical Philosophy* 72 (July / August, 1995), 17–29. Dews argues that 'Žižek is ultimately a "Right Hegelian" masquerading—albeit unwittingly—as a "Left Hegelian"', a philosophical position which is paralled by his 'ambiguous political profile' (26).

Coming to America: Psychoanalytic Criticism in the Age of Žižek

In much of the world, Lacan's ideas for several decades now have had a central, respected place in public discourse: Lacanians write columns in papers and popular magazines, offer their opinions on radio and television talk shows, and of course teach, write, and analyze patients. Lacan is a key part of the curriculum at the most prestigious universities, some of which even grant degrees in Lacanian Theory. In large parts of Europe, South America, Canada, Mexico, Australia, Israel, and elsewhere, Lacan has long been recognized as the most important psychoanalyst after Freud, as the practitioner in whom the Freudian insight is most fully realized and radicalized, and as a thinker whose work continues to be relevant, even urgent, in a wide range of clinical, critical, and political contexts. It is only in the United States that Lacan has been taken up almost exclusively by literary, cultural, and film critics, rather than psychiatrists, philosophers, or social theorists, and then usually in a highly circumscribed way. In recent years, however, America has taken the first steps towards a new encounter with Lacan, one that promises to reveal another, unfamiliar side of psychoanalysis, quite different from the one many people have assumed they knew and have prematurely relegated to the dustbin of history. It is not clear that this resurgence and redirection of interest in Lacan's ideas will spread beyond academia, to the clinic and the public sphere, where it also belongs, but we can make some observations about the transformation of Lacanian studies that is occurring in the U.S. in literary and cultural criticism.

Jacques Lacan first arrived in the United States through the doors of the academy, when in 1966 he came to Baltimore to participate in the symposium 'The Languages of Criticism and the Sciences of Man' at The Johns Hopkins University. This was the occasion of the famous 'Structuralist Controversy,' where America was first exposed not only to Lacan, but also to Jacques Derrida, Roland Barthes, Jean Hyppolite, and several other major French thinkers who would become highly influential in American critical theory over the next three decades. Initially, there was uncertainty as to how to categorize these various writers, all somehow associated, positively or negatively, with the idea of structure; hence American critics embraced the distinction between "structuralism" and 'post-structuralism,' and divided the speakers at the conference into two camps. But Lacan did not seem to fit neatly into either category: was he a high structuralist, like his friend Claude Lévi-Strauss, or to be grouped with deconstruction, which appeared to be the *nouvelle vague*? A Hegelian or a Heideggerian? A Freudian or a post-Freudian? These questions acted as blinkers that for more than twenty years largely prevented America from confronting and coming to productive terms with Lacan. And although many of the exegetical books and essays that came out of the early struggle in America to make sense of Lacan were notable for their readerly care and scholarly effort (viz., the important contributions of Shoshana Felman, Stuart Schneiderman, William Richardson, John P. Muller, Sherry Turkle, Fredric Jameson, and Juliet Flower MacCannell), many were fundamentally misguided and distortive.

Faced with the enormous difficulty of Lacan's writings, perplexed readers often twisted him into ungainly and bizarre shapes that were simply unrecognizable to Lacan's European readers, in the attempt to fit him into a familiar critical box. Some critics fastened onto isolated comments, apparent contradictions, and even textual errata in Lacan's essays, and, pointing to his affiliations with Surrealist artists and poets, concluded that he was intentionally unreadable, meant to derail bourgeois expectations of logic, coherence, and comprehensibility. Others took their lead from the damning accusations of 'logocentrism' and 'phallocentrism' levied against Lacan in France by Derrida, Luce Irigaray, and decided that they didn't need to deal with Lacan at all. Even much of the writing that was sympathetic with Lacan assumed that his work could simply reinforce their pre-existing political beliefs and critical practices, and lend them theoretical weight and authority. At the same time, many of these writers took the rather condescending and patronizing attitude that Lacan, although insightful and useful, is insufficiently radical, hence must be subject to further critique. This lead to a series of narcissistic reimaginings of Lacanian theory in the image of the self, *manqué*: as proto-postcolonialism (although still Eurocentric), as post-structuralism (but insufficiently rigorous), as a fellow traveller of Marxism (but still politically naïve), or as a partner of feminist criticism (although at heart phallocentric and sexist). And Lacan's partisans didn't help matters much by their often hermetic use of Lacanian technical terms and mathemes, which were granted a weight and range of meanings that mystified unconverted readers, leaving them irritated and sceptical. In any case, except for a few notable exceptions, Lacan went largely misread, over-read, or unread in America during the seventies and eighties.

Many factors led to the second wave of Lacanian thinking in the nineties, but the coincidence of two advents made 1989 a signal year for Lacan's American reception: the arrival of Slavoj Žižek and the return of Bruce Fink. After many years in Paris undergoing a training analysis and completing a Ph.D. in the Department of Psychoanalysis at *Paris VIII*, Fink came back to America to practice psychoanalysis, to teach, write, and translate Lacan, first in San Diego and then in Pittsburgh. For the Americans exposed to his writing, his translations and teaching were a revelation: for the first time, Lacan seemed to make sense, to be readable, and not the product of an experiment in automatic writing. The texts that were previously available to monolingual Americans (primarily the abbreviated *Écrits: A Selection* and *Seminar XI: The Four Fundamental Concepts of Psychoanalysis*) were marred by numerous errors and the translators' often limited grasp of the historical trajectory and full range of Lacan's teaching. The result was virtually unreadable texts, even more syntactically questionable than the admittedly dense original. Fink's translations, however, captured Lacan's drift, as well as his tone (often ironic, sometimes mock-pompous, always theatrical); they were never mechanically literal, but aimed at the gist of Lacan's discourse, while remaining precise and idiomatic. Fink's essays on Lacanian concepts and technique were equally lucid, and opened up aspects of Lacan's thought on such topics as alienation and separation, *jouissance*, sexuation, transference, etc. that hadn't been a central part of the American Lacanian discourse. Fink has completed a retranslation of the essays from the American edition of *Écrits* (forthcoming, Norton 2002), and is working on a translation of the entire French volume, which will run to over a thousand pages. When the entire *Écrits* is finally published in English — more than 25 years after its original appearance in French — it will indeed be a watershed event in Lacanian studies in this country. Although this will be far from a 'Standard Edition' of Lacan's *oeuvre* (the principal part of which remains the more than 25 volumes of transcriptions of his annual seminar, most of which have not yet been officially published even in French), for the first time English readers will have available a central complete work by Lacan in an authoritative and annotated translation.

Whereas Fink's crucial contribution has been the production of a readable, reliable text and its articulate exposition, Slavoj Žižek has brought those concepts into remarkably productive relationship with a wide range of other cultural discourses, while injecting a quantum of the disturbing enjoyment that Lacan calls *jouissance* into the critical fields he has opened. The theoretical sophistication, interpretive elegance, and sheer writerly force of Žižek's conjugations of Lacan with philosophy, political theory, and culture in his first English book, *The Sublime Object of Ideology* (Verso, 1989) were unprecedented. The book arrived like a letter bomb that shattered many of our fundamental ideas about Lacan and forced us to reconsider the implications of his work for critical theory and political practice. Most centrally, Žižek's work insisted that the crucial Lacanian opposition was not between the orders of the Imaginary (associated with narcissistic reciprocity and pre-Oedipal totality) and the Symbolic (implying Oedipal substitution, displacement and deferral), but between both those orders, on the one hand, and on the other, the traumatic non-representational enjoyment that Lacan called the Real. Žižek drew special attention to the hideous face of the Real Lacan called, borrowing from Freud and Heidegger, *das Ding*, the alien Thing in-us-more-than-us, the site of primordial horror and the secret source of our *jouissance* that always threatened to emerge from within our most benign fantasies. Although the Thing only appears sporadically in Lacan's seminar and essays, Žižek rightly grants it the primacy usually associated with the *objet a*, which, indeed, is conceptually and genetically its descendant. In Žižek's cultural analyses, the Thing appears in many guises, but it is as 'the enjoyment of the Other' or 'the neighbour's *jouissance*,' that it takes on an explicitly political valence, as the cause of superabundant aggressivity, racism, and xenophobia. As the truth of surplus value as such, the Thing is both the ineluctable basis and intolerable obstacle to all community: the exception understood as the mediating condition of all relationships between universals and particulars.

One element linking Fink and Žižek, and partly accounting for the sympathetic interference of their work, is their common tutelage in the school of Jacques-Alain Miller, Lacan's son-in-law and the director of the psychoanalytic movement most directly connected with his authority, *L'École de la Cause Freudienne* (since 1992 a part of the AMP, the *Association Mondiale de Psychanalyse*, and in its most recent formulation, *l'École Une*). Both Žižek and Fink developed their approaches to Lacan in Jacques-Alain Miller's famously lucid seminar and through their experience of analysis with Miller; they have both extensively acknowledged their debt to Miller, and emphasized the degree to which Lacan's thinking cannot be disimbricated from Miller's. Miller's appropriation of Lacan is controversial: for many people, his control of Lacan's *oeuvre* (he has absolute editorial power over all publication of Lacan's work, and is technically the co-author of the Seminar, where the frontispiece announces that the text has been 'established' by Jacques-Alain Miller) translates into the desire to control Lacan's meaning. And there is no doubt that he is deeply interested in having Lacan's work be understood as infinitely complex, contradictory, but nevertheless fundamentally coherent. But, whether they love him or hate him, it is arguable that there is no Lacanian who has not learned most of what he or she knows about Lacan from Miller, directly or indirectly. And this is not merely to say that Miller's approach to Lacan is the most persuasive and influential, because of its remarkably synthetic vision, striking clarity, powerful formalizations, etc. (although all this is true). Rather, Miller's ideas are grafted onto Lacan's in an absolutely unique way, *transforming* Lacan's thinking in ways that Lacan explicitly endorsed. From Lacan's 1964 seminar on *The Four Fundamental Concepts of Psychoanalysis*, Miller was a constant participant in Lacan's seminar, and increasingly his collaborator in publishing and teaching. There is, however, nothing sycophantic about Miller's relationship to Lacan; he was Lacan's interlocutor, but one who could take the role of an inquisitor, insisting on clarity, holding Lacan accountable for everything he said, or goading him with sceptical doubts from the position of Devil's Advocate. In the epigraph to *Television*, the transcript of an interview Miller conducted with Lacan on French television in 1973, Lacan wrote (clearly referring to Miller); 'He who interrogates me also knows how to read me'. With Lacan's death in 1981, Miller began teaching his own seminar, and like Lacan, teaching, rather than publishing, has been the central forum for the transmission of his ideas.

Whereas the American understanding of Lacan had previously been guided by readings and misreadings of those few of his essays that had been translated in *Écrits: A Selection*, Fink and Žižek were drawing on the full range of Lacan's work and thought, and on their experience of the theoretical clarity that is the hallmark of the French clinical orientation to psychoanalysis. Lacan's *Écrits* had been published in France in 1966, and the latest essay in the truncated American edition was written in 1960, based on a seminar from 1957–58, whereas Lacan went on to write and teach for another fifteen years, and arguably produced his most important ideas in those later years. Although one can manufacture a hologrammatic account of Lacan, where all aspects of his thinking can be read in any of its parts or moments, it seems clear that his work underwent a shift in conceptual emphasis and ethical valence in the 1960s, from an imperative for the symbolic over the imaginary, to one for the real. From the expanded perspectives provided by the Seminars and the clinic, an entirely different Lacan emerges, one who has very little to do with the questions posed by structuralism or its aftermath. And when Fink and Žižek brought that Lacan to America, it seemed both rich and strange, startlingly unfamiliar and offering an unprecedented wealth of new possibilities for American critical and clinical appropriation.

In many ways, the early phase of the Americanization of Lacan was a repetition of the original American reception of psychoanalysis: when Freud came to America for the first time in the 30s, he knew that the psychoanalytic *aperçu* would likely be misrecognized as a panacea; as he is reported to have remarked to Jung, 'They don't know it, but we bring them the plague'. What Freud didn't know, of course, was how easily America would be able to defend itself against the difficult, disturbing insights of psychoanalysis and convert it into another version of 'the American way of life,' most notably in the invention of Ego Psychology, which would endorse a notion of the self as the accumulation of narcissistic capital. In a sense, what Žižek has done is to restore the *virulence* of the psychoanalytic plague, to dredge up what had been filtered out in the American reception of Lacan. The point is, before Žižek *we had not yet begun to encounter Lacan in this country*, we had prematurely turned away or presumed we understood what we had not yet faced, and what we have yet to fully confront. And it is only now, through Žižek's work, that we are beginning to think the specificity of psychoanalysis itself.

It is easy to assume that "authentic" psychoanalysis is only psycho-analysis in the clinic, on the couch; and, indeed, this attitude characterizes much of the French condescension for American Laca-nianism, and its primarily academic source and audience. The French tend to categorize all American writing on or with Lacan (even in its more rigorous, Žižekian manifestations) as "cultural studies", hence, whatever merits it might have or however insightful it might occasionally be, as "not psychoanalysis". Psychoanalysis, they insist, is an experience between an analyst and an analysand, and has nothing to do with movies, books, or other cultural productions. But what Žižek's work has made clear (and here I also mean his work as a synecdoche for much of the work he has inspired), above all, is that psychoanalysis is *primarily* imbricated with other discourses, centrally art, philosophy, science, and religion. The insistence on encountering the question "what is psychoanalysis *in itself*?", which is of course crucial, and cannot be thought in exclusion of the question of the clinic, should not be misunderstood as a call to discursive isolationism: both Freud and Lacan position psychoanalysis as a border concept, one whose specificity arises precisely in the intersection and gaps between other discourses. Hence, when Freud or Lacan examine an artwork like *Hamlet*, this should not be mistaken as an extra-curricular foray of psychoanalysis into literary criticism, but as a suggestion that some element of psychoanalysis itself *necessarily* arises and coalesces in the field of literature, according to distinctly literary logics and systems of transmission. The same can be said about religious texts, such as the Biblical injunction to 'love thy neighbor as thyself': something *primary* to psychoanalysis comes into being in its commentaries on religion, even if Freud and Lacan personally were both staunchly secular. Certainly, much of the critical appropriation of Lacan in America, even after Žižek, has been merely "cultural studies", that is, has failed to comprehend the specificity of psychoanalysis in its facile application of some fragment of Lacan's thought or vocabulary to cultural questions that remain fundamentally un-psychoanalytic. But since Shoshana Felman's famous introduction, 'To Open the Question,' the distinction between the critical applications of psychoanalytic theory to cultural artifacts and the more radical *implications* that psychoanalysis may have for criticism has been available in the American academy, and crucial to many of its most insightful and radical thinkers.

Žižek's work has made the point for the first time in America that, by bringing out the most profound implications of Freud's discovery, Lacan's work represented a coherent, and indeed *rigorous* account of psychoanalysis, one that did not reflect simple preconceived ideas about the nature of psychoanalysis or contemporary French critical thought. Moreover, the genius of Žižek's contribution was to demonstrate that this version of Lacan offered an extraordinarily fruitful approach to thought, culture, and religion. No longer was Lacan up for grabs, subject to endless reinvention in the image of his readers; no more would graduate students and professors sit in seminars and reading groups and dream up baroque theories about what Lacan meant by such terms or 'mathemes' as the subject, the Other, and the *objet a*, for now we had trustworthy guides to show us paths and clearings in the thicket. And along with this clarification came an enormously expanded sense of possibilities: through Fink's translations and explanations, Lacan's work gained new clinical significance and usefulness; and through the seductive wit and brilliance of Žižek's writings and the sheer force of his personal presence, Lacan suddenly seemed not only *useful* but *singular* and *urgent*, the purveyor of a truth not otherwise available, and perhaps most surprisingly, unembarrassed by the idea of 'the truth,' not committed to the dogmatic slumber of a relativism that seemed to have become academia's postmodern *lingua franca* and most fundamental point of common assumption.

What are the fundamental concepts or logics in Lacan that Žižek's work brings to bear on philosophy, politics, and culture? What is it in Lacan that had been so systematically missed in America before Žižek? First of all, the notion that psychoanalysis does not constitute a body of concepts, definitions, and dogmas so much as a unique *rupture* in the history of conceptualization, definition, and dogmatism, of *theory* as such. But what is the nature of this cut or wound in the western episteme introduced by Freud and probed and deepened by Lacan? In what sense is psychoanalysis fundamentally incomparable, its paradigms incompatible with those of other postmodern discourses? We have barely begun to comprehend the nature of this rupture, yet its consequences, political, social, and clinical, are increasingly evident and exigent everywhere in the world today.

To pose these questions, however, is not to call for a return to a Freudian orthodoxy made available by Lacanian rigour. It is time now neither for the deconstruction nor reconstruction of psychoanalysis, but for what we might call its *construction*, in a precise psychoanalytic sense of that term. In Freud's famous late essay, 'Constructions in Analysis' (1937), he distinguishes between the work of 'interpretation,' which outlines the structure of the unconscious by painstakingly following its movement from one signifying element to the next, and 'construction,' as an analytic technique that aims to *intervene in* the structure of the unconscious. An analytic construction may be inaccurate, patently fictitious, even absurd, at the level of symbolic and imaginary meanings, for it aims at the sublime truth of the *real*, resistant to all representation. As Freud puts it, construction is the 'bait of falsehood' that takes 'a carp of truth'. Such a work of construction understands its project not only as exegetical or hermeneutical, but as theoretical and practical interventions in the fundamental fantasies that determine our world. And this is why America is a privileged object of Lacanian Critical Theory, insofar as the United States has a unique and strategically crucial role in world fantasy. The United States remains "unanalyzed", both in the sense that it has domesticated the disturbing insights of psychoanalysis into the anodyne ideology of 'The American Way of Life' and insofar as it remains an enigmatic object in world desire, the object of simultaneous envy and derision, love and hate. The concept of 'construction' has none of the distance implicit in the deconstructive expression (borrowed from Heidegger) of putting a term 'under erasure' — that is, to both use it and disavow it, acknowledging its metaphysical roots but finding no other satisfactory vocabulary. To place psychoanalysis *under construction* is not to 'reconstruct' it, to rehabilitate its embarrassing slips or apparent anachronisms, its blindspot and residues of distasteful ideology, but to locate oneself squarely and unapologetically in the Freudian field, as a work in progress, an incomplete gesture, an unfolding drama, an explosion whose first flash has blinded us to its real impact, with which we have not yet fully come to terms. We must be willing to not take psychoanalysis for granted, as theory, technique, or interpretive methodology, but take on the challenge of reading Freud and Lacan *as if for the first time*.

KENNETH REINHARD
UCLA

Notes on Contributors

Terry Eagleton is Professor of Cultural Theory at Manchester University, author of about twenty-five works of literary criticism and cultural theory, as well as of plays produced in Ireland and London.

Jerry Aline Flieger is Professor of French, Comparative Literature and Theory, and Women's Studies at Rutgers University. She has taught and lectured worldwide on psychoanalysis and millennial culture, and is currently national Chair of the MLA Division on Psychological Approaches to Literature. Her work has appeared in numerous international collections on psychoanalysis and theory, and in journals such as *PMLA, Diacritics, New Literary History, Sub-stance, South Atlantic Quarterly, MLN,* and *Pre-textes.* She is the author of *The Purloined Punchline: Freud's Comic Theory and the Postmodern Text* (Johns Hopkins UP, 1990); *Colette and the Fantom Subject of Autobiography* (Cornell UP, 1991), and a forthcoming work on millennial theory: *Is Oedipus Online?: Siting Freud in the Posthuman Century.*

Jason Glynos is a lecturer in political theory at the Department of Government, University of Essex. His research and publications explore and develop discourse analytic and psychoanalytic approaches to social and political analysis, focusing on issues of identity construction and theories of ideology and democracy. He is co-editor of *Lacan & Science* (forthcoming).

Russell Grigg teaches philosophy and psychoanalytic studies at Deakin University. He is a member of the École de la Cause freudienne and the Lacan Circle of Melbourne, and practices psychoanalysis in Melbourne. He is the translator of Lacan's *Seminar III, The Psychoses* (Norton, 1993) and *Seminar XVII, The Other Side of Psychoanalysis* (Norton, forthcoming).

Michael Moriarty is Professor of French Literature and Thought at Queen Mary, University of London. He is the author *of Taste and Ideology in Seventeenth-Century France* (Cambridge: CUP, 1988) and *Roland Barthes* (Cambridge: Polity, 1991).

Bran Nicol was educated at the universities of Dundee and Lancaster. He is currently a lecturer in the School of English at University College, Chichester, where he is also involved in the Centre for

Contemporary Critical Thought. His publications include books on Iris Murdoch and D.M. Thomas and the forthcoming Reader *Postmodernism and the Contemporary Novel* (Edinburgh University Press).

Kenneth Reinhard is Associate Professor of English and Comparative Literature at UCLA and the Director of the UCLA Center for Jewish Studies. He is a founder and member of the Central Committee of the American Lacanian Link. He has published essays on Freud, Lacan, Levinas, Henry James, and the Bible, and co-wrote *After Oedipus: Shakespeare in Psychoanalysis* (Cornell UP, 1993) with Julia Reinhard Lupton. He is currently completing a book for Princeton University Press on the Ethics of the Neighbor in religion, philosophy, and psychoanalysis.

Edmond Wright is a member of the Philosophy Faculty, University of Cambridge, and a sometime Researcher at the Swedish Collegium for Advanced Study of the Social Sciences at Uppsala. He publishes regularly in the philosophical journals on language, perception, and epistemology. He is the editor of *The Ironic Discourse* (*Poetics Today*, 1983), *New Representationalisms: Essays In The Philosophy Of Perception* (Avebury, 1993) and co-editor of *The Žižek Reader* (Blackwell, 1999).

Slavoj Žižek, philosopher and psychoanalyst, Senior Researcher at the Kulturwissenschaftliches Institut, Essen. Latest publications: *The Fragile Absolute* (London 2000), *Did Somebody Say Totalitarianism?* (London 2001).